CERAMIC SKILLBOOKS

Series Editor:
Murray Fieldhouse

Electric Kilns and Firing

H. Fraser, F.I.Ceram, A.M.Inst. Ref. Eng.

PITMAN

PITMAN PUBLISHING LIMITED
39 Parker Street, London WC2B 5PB

Associated Companies
Copp Clark Pitman, Toronto
Fearon Pitman Inc, San Francisco
Pitman Publishing New Zealand Ltd, Wellington
Pitman Publishing Pty Ltd, Melbourne

Originally published as *Kilns and Kiln Firing for the Craft
Potter* 1969. This new revised edition first published 1980.

© Pitman Publishing 1979

ISBN 0 273 01393 9 (cased edition)
ISBN 0 273 01394 7 (paperback edition)

Text set in 10/12 pt IBM Century, printed by photolithography, and
bound in Great Britain at The Pitman Press, Bath

Contents

Acknowledgements

My thanks are due to the following companies who have so kindly provided information or photographs used in the compilation of this book —
Potclays Ltd, Kilns and Furnaces Ltd, Ether Instruments Ltd, Podmore & Sons Ltd, Wengers Ltd, Sangamo Weston Ltd.
Also to the College of Earth and Mineral Sciences, Pennsylvania State University, and to David Lewis for his encouragement, without which this book might not have been completed.

This book is dedicated to Helen.

Preface

This coming winter hundreds of evening institutes in towns and villages throughout the country will introduce pottery making into their curriculum and by so doing will swell the ranks of the thousands whose courses are already well established. This is testimony to the considerable growth in recent years of pottery as a craft.

This awakening of latent interest in pottery making has been precipitated by several factors but one of the most important of these has been the development of a range of studio electric kilns specially designed to meet the needs of the craft — and at prices within the reach of all. Nevertheless, despite the tremendous appeal and convenience of the modern studio kiln, it still tends to be regarded with awe by most potters and teachers faced with a need to use a kiln for the first time. For some reason its correct operation is thought to result only from years of training and experience — and a measure of inspired intuition.

Pottery firing is not quite so simple as some experts would have us believe but, on the other hand, there is no 'magic' in the process and certainly, there is nothing that should daunt anyone given a little knowledge of the procedures involved. Successful firing mainly comes from an understanding of what happens when ceramic materials are heated, a knowledge of the firing requirements of the products to be fired, and an ability to control the temperature, time-cycle and kiln atmosphere by regulation of a few simple controls.

I hope that this book assists in supplying this basic knowledge and thus enables the novice to fire a kiln with complete assurance and satisfaction.

There should be much here, too, for the teacher or more advanced potter who may find those chapters on kiln instrumentation, effect of heat on clays and glazes, etc., of particular interest.

1 Kiln Construction and Design

The design and construction of studio pottery kilns has entailed a great deal of careful planning. Perfection can seldom be achieved without simplicity but this apparent simplicity of the craft pottery kiln is very misleading. The basic structure of each kiln — particularly of those offered by reputable suppliers — is generally carefully designed to give adequate strength to withstand movement and knocks without being clumsy and excessively heavy. The type of refractory insulation brickwork used in kiln construction is carefully selected and may vary from one size of kiln to another, depending upon the type and thickness of brickwork necessary to reduce heat losses to acceptable limits. The position and optimum size of vent holes, etc., is determined only after careful research and calculation, in order that the firing performance remains quite satisfactory. The bricks themselves have to be well fitted together if the kiln is to give long service, and carefully shaped around the door if the door is to give a snug fit so as to prevent excessive heat losses. Element design and layout is likewise very much a part of the technology of kiln construction if optimum results are to be obtained. A very great deal of thought, calculation and research, as well as a considerable amount of trial and error, have gone into the construction of the modern efficient craft pottery kiln and it is this careful attention to detail that has produced kilns that provide efficiency and long life with freedom from continual maintenance.

In kiln construction the framework is built first and then the brickwork is built within the frame, the electrical fitments and elements being added afterwards.

Framework

This is normally built of angle-section steel, although in smaller kilns the framework may be made from strip steel or pressed steel panels. Angle-section steel is, however, particularly useful as a basis for building in the brickwork as this section gives support on two sides. All joints are normally welded together but the sheet panelling can be fixed with screws or bolts. A photograph of a typical framework assembly is given in Fig. 1.

Brickwork

The two types of bricks used generally for the construction of kilns are refractory bricks and refractory insulation bricks and

Fig. 1 Typical steel cabinet used as a base structure for craft pottery kiln. *Courtesy of Kilns and Furnaces Ltd.*

they should not be confused. Refractory bricks are normally fairly dense bricks and are, therefore, comparatively heavy in weight. They absorb heat fairly quickly and if one face of the brick is exposed to heat the other side of the brick will very soon become warm as the heat is conducted through the brick.

Fig. 2 Kiln and stand utilising angle-iron frame. The handwheel on the door is a power interlock device to isolate power whenever the door is open.
Courtesy of Cromartie Kilns Ltd.

Refractory bricks, therefore, tend to be used in those positions where heat loss is not quite so important — for example, for the building of chimneys or for the exterior brickwork of oil or gas fired kilns. This type of brick is seldom used in the manufacture of electric kilns, due to this high heat conductivity and the considerable weight which would make carriage charges more expensive and movement of the kiln more difficult.

Instead, bricks of the refractory insulation type are used: these have all the heat-resisting qualities of refractory bricks but are very porous indeed. Air, as we all know, is a good insulator and the huge number of air pockets inside these bricks makes them good insulators of heat so that if one face of the brick is exposed to heat it takes a considerable time before this heat is transmitted through the brick to the opposite face. This pore structure makes the bricks very light in weight.

The very high porosity (i.e. pore structure) gives another very useful property to these bricks; i.e. it makes them comparatively soft and easy to cut with a normal hacksaw. They can therefore be very easily shaped so that cutting a groove to take elements, or boring holes in them, presents no problem.

The brickwork is built into the framework using a heat-resisting compound of a similar composition to the bricks themselves. Care is taken to make the joints as fine as possible since large gaps between bricks filled with jointing compound are unsightly in appearance and a possible source of weakness.

Ceramic fibre
This remarkable material has become an increasingly common kiln insulant in the last ten years or so because of its combination of refractoriness, low weight and phenomenal insulation properties. Kilns incorporating ceramic fibre insulation — often referred to as 'low thermal mass' kilns — use up much less of the generated heat thus resulting in low firing costs and permitting larger kiln capacities for the same electrical loading. Since less thickness of insulation is needed, the kiln weight can be reduced. A problem, however, is that it has poor strength and abrasion resistance and so it is often used as a hot-face insulant with conventional refractory insulation bricks used as back-up insulation and as corner posts. The elements are generally

supported by rods passed through them or by some other means to prevent the ceramic fibre from bearing the weight.

Durability and structural problems tend to restrict significant economies to semi-industrial kilns and particularly where fast turn-round times are needed (for low thermal mass kilns tend to cool very rapidly). It is not unusual for decorating kilns utilising ceramic fibre to be fired three times per day.

Electrical wiring and fitments

With most designs of kilns the 'works' such as junction boxes, terminals, etc., are fitted at the back of the kiln and access to them can normally be gained by removing a panel from the kiln. Electric kilns, of course, take quite a considerable current — especially the larger sizes — and when the kilns are switched on and off the switching device must be robust to withstand the sparking which may occur. The switching is therefore often done through a contactor, which is merely a robust relay enabling the kiln to be switched on and off without burning away any of the connexions, etc. Smaller kilns may not be fitted with a contactor and this is why one is normally required if any form of energy regulator is subsequently fitted to the kiln, for these energy regulators operate by continually switching the kiln on and off.

Electricity supply to each element is normally made through a small brass connector. Steel connectors tend to oxidise too readily.

Some kilns are fitted as standard with an energy regulator complete with a little pilot light which is switched automatically on and off as the energy regulator switches the current to the elements on and off. A few kilns are fitted with a door switch as a standard item — particularly where the kiln is to be used for metal enamelling. The majority of kilns used by the craft and school potter are, however, merely fitted with a rotary switch which normally has four settings marked upon it, denoted 'Off', 'Low', 'Medium' and 'High'. These settings refer to the amount of current which is allowed to flow to the elements and thus the rate at which the kiln increases its temperature.

Usually the kiln is fitted with a control panel — rather like the dashboard of a motor car — on which the electrical accessories mentioned above are fitted. Some kilns, however, are supplied

Fig. 3 Brass connectors used for element connection.

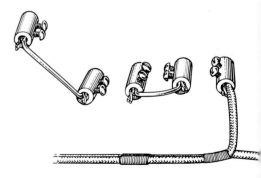

with a separate control panel which has to be mounted on an adjacent wall or other convenient surface.

Following the Health and Safety at Work Act, it is now demanded that a kiln be fitted with a 'power interlock'. This can be either a captive key type interlock (such as the Castell type) using an isolator for the mains input, or a 'fail to safety' door switch can be used provided the switch positively isolates the mains power rather than with a contactor. The latter is common practice on kilns up to 3kw rating, single phase (i.e. will operate off a 13 or 15 amp socket). These devices ensure that once a firing is commenced the kiln door cannot be opened without the electricity supply being switched off.

Additionally, some manufacturers make provision for a padlock to be fitted to the door so that the door cannot be opened without removing the padlock.

Elements

There are several types of elements which can be fitted to kilns, but the most popular types are those known as Kanthal A and Kanthal A1 elements; Kanthal DSD is widely used up to $1200°C$. Other types of elements, such as Nichrome, Super Kanthal or silicon carbide, can also be fitted. Let us now look at each of these element types in turn.

Nichrome elements
These, as the name implies, are made basically from an alloy of nickel and chromium and are fitted to kilns which are not required to operate at temperatures above about $1050°C$. The fitting of these elements may enable a kiln to attain temperatures up to $1150°C$ but at temperatures as high as this the elements would very quickly burn away and so for all practical purposes the maximum temperature is normally kept down to $1000°C$ or thereabouts. This temperature, however, is quite sufficient for enamelling, biscuiting and low-temperature glazes. Nichrome wire is comparatively cheap and is, incidentally, the wire used for domestic electric fires. One cannot, however, use the wire from a domestic fire in one of these kilns for within the enclosed kiln such wire would very quickly burn away. A free flow of air around electric-fire elements helps to keep the actual element

temperature within reasonable limits. This would not happen inside a kiln.

Kanthal A and A1 elements

These are made from alloys of iron, aluminium, chromium and cobalt and it is claimed that these alloys will give three times the life of the Nichrome types at similar temperatures. These alloys do not contain nickel and the great disadvantage is that once they have been fired they become very brittle and have to be well supported in the kiln. Any knocks or shaking can easily break them at this stage. Kanthal A or Kanthal DSD elements will allow the kiln to reach maximum temperatures of about 1200°C but Kanthal A1 elements will allow a maximum operating temperature of 1300°C. These are the types of elements most commonly used in electric kilns. An important feature of Kanthal wire is that after firing, the wire becomes coated with aluminium oxide, which protects the wire from attack by most of the harmful gases. Exposure to reducing atmospheres will, however, very quickly remove this coating and the elements will then deteriorate very quickly unless the coating is restored by an oxidising fire. Alkali vapours and halogen vapours — for example, fluorine, iodine, etc. — are harmful to elements and so is lead vapour. Kanthal wire is not attacked by sulphur compounds as is Nichrome wire.

Super Kanthal and silicon carbide elements

These are used only for very high-temperature work beyond the temperatures used in pottery production. Temperatures of 1600°C can be attained with Super Kanthal and 1500°C with silicon carbide. Both types of elements are very expensive and as the resistance of the silicon carbide elements increases with each firing, voltage regulators have to be fitted. Both types are normally used only for industrial applications.

Elements of the Nichrome and Kanthal types are wound into a continuous spiral which is usually formed into a hairpin shape, i.e. two rows of element coils joined at one end. The last six to nine inches of each end of the element is not coiled but is left as a straight wire so that these element 'tails', as they are called, can be pushed through holes drilled through the rear wall of the kiln and fastened to brass connectors in the connexion chamber at the rear of the kiln.

The determination of the correct amount of element wire to use for the elements is part of the science of kiln technology and is thus one of the more difficult problems which face the 'do-it-yourself' enthusiast. Not only does the kiln technologist calculate how much wire of a certain grade is needed to supply the necessary amount of heat for a given kiln size, he also has to adjust his data to conform to different voltages and he has to calculate the number of coils into which the elements must be made — which must be within certain limits if optimum element life is to be obtained.

Most high-temperature kilns are designed to give a very even temperature distribution at around 1100°C. At temperatures above and below this point there tends to be an increasing degree of temperature variation. In an attempt to obtain the least possible variation over a wide range of temperature, some kiln manufacturers fit graded elements into their kilns. This does have the slight disadvantage that it is not possible to keep one spare element to guard against a risk of element failure since one does not know which element will fail first, but this disadvantage is more than compensated by the more even firing characteristics.

An alternative way to obtain an even temperature distribution over the complete firing cycle is to wire the elements into groups or 'banks' and to fit an independent energy regulator to control each bank of elements. Two or three thermocouples are then fitted to the kiln, so that if the temperature in one part of the kiln shows signs of lagging behind the rest of the kiln, the energy regulator controlling the elements in that region can be turned to a higher setting so that more heat is introduced. This system is often used with large studio and semi-industrial kilns but is not customary with the kilns more commonly used by craft and school potters because of the expense involved.

The vast majority of craft pottery kilns are of the exposed element type. This means that the elements are supported in grooves or channels cut into the walls of the kiln leaving the elements clearly visible. This method is much cheaper, more efficient, and lends itself to easier maintenance, than the alternative muffle type of kiln in which the elements are completely hidden from sight behind a thin wall of refractory

Fig. 4 36″ high vase by Michael Hawkins, fired in an electric kiln to 1275°C oxidation. Made from Pyropot clay with sgraffito decoration.

material made of sillimanite or, better still, of silicon carbide (Carborundum), through which the heat has to pass to reach the ware.

If ever it is necessary to replace a burnt-out element, always quote the serial number of your kiln to the kiln manufacturer, indicating which particular element has failed, and always make certain that *every* trace of the burnt-out element has been removed from the element grooves before fitting the replacement. This is most important. When fitting a replacement element also ensure that the screws holding the element tails into the connectors are as tight as you can get them, so as to prevent sparking which creates a hot spot which can burn through the element. Once the element tails are secured, the element is then stretched over the grooves and thus fitted into place. Don't stretch the element before fitting the tails into position for if it is overstretched in this way it will not fit into its grooves sufficiently tightly and eventually will lead to part of the element escaping from the groove.

Incidentally, if a Kanthal element burns through at the connector, it is often possible to stretch the element a little so as to be able to reconnect it by strongly heating part of the element inside the kiln (close to the element tail) in a blow-torch flame, whilst pulling the wire gently from the rear connexion chamber. Naturally, any attempt to do this whilst the element is cool would probably result in breakage, since Kanthal wires become brittle after a few firings, but at high temperatures they are always soft.

The first firing

Before any kiln is put into use, it should be fired slowly to a temperature no higher than 100 or 200 degrees below the maximum firing temperature for which it was designed. This gentle firing drives away any moisture present in the brickwork, after which the kiln is ready to be put into full service.

With a kiln capable of firing to 1300°C for example, a good general procedure might be to fire at about 75°C per hour (regulator on 'low' or about 30—50) with the vent hole open up to 450—500°C (black heat) and then to hold temperature at this point for approximately two hours. Increase temperature at 75°C per hour up to about 800—900°C (cherry red) or until a little steam is visibly escaping from the kiln at which point the vent plug can be replaced. The regulator is then set to high or 100 and the temperature taken up to 1100—1150°C (light orange) at which point it is held for one hour and the kiln is then shut off.

As an alternative, one manufacturer recommends a slow firing up to 500°C with the vent open and then holding temperature for about eight hours. Whichever method is adopted, two factors are important:

Firstly, if large volumes of steam are escaping from the kiln it is best to hold the temperature steady until this has been reduced.

Secondly, one has some opportunity of checking to see that the pyrometer (if fitted) is functioning correctly. In any event, never rely absolutely upon a pyrometer for any firing until you have checked that it is reading correctly.

After this first firing has taken place, it may be noticed that a few fine cracks have formed in the interior brickwork of the kiln. These cracks will close up when the kiln is next heated and open up again when the kiln is subsequently cooled. They therefore serve as expansion joints and are in no way detrimental to the operation of the kiln. During the initial firings a paint odour may be detected. This also can be ignored as it is inevitable and will disappear after a few firings.

Some other factors

Electricity supplies

Kilns having a rating of less than 6·75 kilowatts can generally be installed into domestic situations without undue difficulty since they will consume about 28 amps on full load from a 240 volt electricity supply — and houses in the UK are usually fused to accept up to 30 amps on the cooker and immersion heater circuits. The actual supply to the house may be 60 amps or perhaps 100 amps and provided that electricity is not in use for heating and cooking, kilns of 12kw or more can be installed. Kilns of a rating larger than the house supplies can accommodate will demand that extra power supplies be installed to the premises. This may or may not be expensive.

Much depends upon the capacity of the existing supply, the availability of additional supply if needed, and upon the current consumed on the premises by other electrical apparatus. The prospective buyer is therefore recommended to contact the local Electricity Board who would always be prepared to advise given an indication of the kilowatt rating proposed.

Cost of firing

This can be approximated by multiplying the kilowatt rating by the cost of one unit of electricity and multiplying this by the length of time required to fire the kiln before switching off.

For example, a 6kw kiln operating from a supply costing, say, 3 pence per unit of electricity and firing for ten hours would give a maximum cost of $6 \times 3 \times 10 = £1.80$ per firing. This calculation presumes, however, that the kiln is switched to its maximum setting for the full ten hours but this would not, of course, normally be the case and so the firing cost would be less than that indicated.

Routine maintenance
Try to keep the inside of the kiln and the element grooves as clean as possible by using a vacuum cleaner when necessary.

Any small chips from brickwork — perhaps resulting from the digging out of a spot of molten metal when changing elements — can be filled using high temperature refractory insulation cement. Larger repairs demand shaping the hole to take a piece fashioned from a spare refractory insulation brick and sticking this into position with refractory insulation cement.

Every six to twelve months check to see that the vent plug is seating properly and that all element connectors are tight and uncorroded. Make sure that the mains electricity is isolated before doing the latter!

2 Kiln Accessories and Instrumentation

There are many different types of 'extras' which can be fitted to pottery kilns, some of which are standard fitments of certain models produced by some manufacturers. The more popular ones are detailed below.

The rotary switch

Some provision for varying the rate of temperature increase of a pottery kiln is more or less essential. The rotary switch, otherwise known as a three-position or four-position switch, is the simplest way of providing this service, and many craft pottery kilns are therefore fitted with one of these by the manufacturer.

The switch itself has four positions only at which it can be set. These positions are generally indicated by the words 'Off', 'Low', 'Medium' and 'High'. These settings refer to the rate at which the kiln will increase its temperature.

The switch is usually wired in what is referred to as a 'series/parallel' circuit, which is an electrical way of varying the manner in which the elements are wired into the mains supply at each position of the switch. This effectively changes the amount of heat generated by the elements at each setting.

As the electricity supply is not switched on and off to retard the temperature rise, as is done with an energy regulator, a contactor is not required.

With most kilns the operation is such that when the switch is set at its 'low' setting the energized elements do not actually glow, as does an electric fire, but remain at 'black heat'.

Energy regulator

This is purely a retarding medium for controlling the rate of temperature increase, which it does by controlling the heat input to the kiln. It comprises an automatic switching device, the time periods during which the switch contacts are open and closed being infinitely variable. The length of time during which the contacts are closed is controlled by an adjusting knob which is usually calibrated from 0 to 100 per cent. When the knob is set to its 100 per cent setting the contacts are closed all the time and so the electricity supply to the elements is never interrupted, the kiln therefore heating up at its maximum rate.

Fig. 5. Sunvic energy regulator (housed in panel with indicator lights and slidelock fuse).

The energy regulator is mounted either on the kiln or on a separate control panel unit which can be mounted adjacent to the kiln. A small indicator light is often incorporated into the regulator and this switches on when the regulator switch contacts are closed and switches off again when the contacts open. When the kiln elements are receiving electricity supply the indicator light therefore lights up and switches off again when the element supply is cut off.

An energy regulator is a very useful piece of equipment as the rate of temperature increase can be controlled so easily. Thus if thick-walled pots are being fired the rate of temperature increase can very easily be reduced. If a pyrometer is fitted to the kiln and one wished to maintain the kiln at a particular temperature, the energy regulator setting could be adjusted until a position was found at which the elements were switched on and off at a rate slow enough to prevent any further temperature rise but fast enough to prevent the temperature from dropping. This procedure, however, should only be done for short periods as otherwise the temperature may begin to drift.

There is a type of energy regulator known as a Simmerstat which is often fitted to kilns. However, the lowest setting of a Simmerstat control allows an appreciably faster rate of temperature increase than one would obtain from the lowest setting of the standard Sunvic form of energy regulator, the Sunvic type of energy regulator giving a wider range of control. Simmerstats are frequently used on small test kilns operating from 13 amp plug sockets since they can switch up to 13 amps without needing a relay.

Door switch

This device, which isolates the electrical supply to the elements when the kiln door is opened, will be encountered on many kilns. Prior to 1975 the usual type consisted of a switch which was actuated by a bracket on the kiln door which depressed a spring-loaded plunger when the door was brought to its closed position. The plunger operated switch in turn actuated the contactor relay which allowed current to flow to the kiln elements. Upon opening the door the plunger was released, thus isolating the supply via the contactor relay. Following the

Health and Safety at Work Act however, the fitment of such door switches is no longer considered an adequate safeguard since there is always an electrical supply to one side of the door switch even when the door is open: thus the kiln is not completely isolated.

It should be remembered that, with most kilns, the elements do not begin to glow for an appreciable number of seconds after the kiln has been switched on even if the kiln energy regulator is set at its highest setting. Indeed, if a rotary switch only is fitted and this is set at its low position, the elements may never glow but remain at black heat. Under these conditions, the risk of electrocution arising from a child opening the door and perhaps accidentally touching the elements must not be overlooked. Consequently, some way of safely and automatically isolating the electrical supply when the door is opened is a valuable safeguard — and a mandatory one following the 1975 Act.

The situation now is that with kilns which switch less than 3kw, single phase, a fail-safe door switch can be used provided that this positively isolates the supply rather than operating through a relay. Kilns greater than 3kw rating demand a purpose-built fail-safe door switch or a trapped-key interlock system of which there are several makes, the most popular in the UK probably being the Castell interlock.

Trapped key interlock (Castell lock etc.)

This simple but ingenious device comprises a door bolt which is locked home by means of a key and an electricity switchbox operated by the same key. Only after firmly closing the kiln door and locking the bolt can the key be withdrawn to put into the switchbox to switch on power to the kiln. Furthermore, the key cannot be withdrawn from the switchbox to unlock the kiln door until the power is switched off first. Thus the key is either trapped in the kiln door lock (power off) or trapped in the switchbox (power on; door closed).

Trapped key interlocks are generally used in conjunction with a contactor relay but the general principle holds that when the kiln door is open there is no electrical supply to the kiln or its accessories.

Heat fuse

This is a fusible link which is fitted into a kiln in a similar manner to a thermocouple, i.e. with a part of it projecting into the kiln firing chamber. Heat fuses are manufactured to conform to a wide range of individual temperatures and when this temperature is reached the heat fuse melts, thus breaking a circuit and cutting off the supply to the kiln.

Heat fuses are not used to control the end point of a kiln firing but are used as a safety valve to cut off the power supply when the temperature for some reason reaches a level at which damage is likely to result. Fuses to melt at about 1350°C are often fitted for example to kilns being fired up to 1300°C, as 1350°C is beyond the maximum temperature at which the pottery is fired, but below the point at which temperature damage to the bricks or shelves is likely to result.

Fig. 6 Heat fuse.

Time switch

There are, of course, many different types of time switches differing in size and complexity. Generally they are fitted with a time scale graduated with twenty-four hourly divisions, each division normally being sub-divided still further into proportions of one hour. Two separate pointers are normally fitted alongside the scale, the pointers being movable so that they can be set to any desired setting. When the electricity supply is switched on, the time switch begins to operate like a clock and will automatically operate a relay to switch on the kiln when the time indicated by one of the two pointers reaches a certain reference point which denotes the actual time of day. The kiln will then be switched off when the second pointer reaches the reference point. In addition to this, certain models can be programmed to operate at the required times on a required day, i.e. they have day control in addition to hour control.

Fig. 7 Time switch set to switch on at 2.30 p.m. and off again at 2.15 a.m.
Courtesy of Sangamo Western Ltd.

Time switches can be useful under certain circumstances but one must remember that the length of time taken for any firing will vary from one firing to the next depending upon the variation in the amount of ware inside the kiln and in the voltage of the electricity supply for example.

Some years ago I carried out many firings at RAF Marham, in Norfolk, with a small kiln fitted with a time switch. I found the

Fig. 8 'Tall chamber' electric kiln fitted with Castel Lock on the door and Sunvic regulator on the panel. *Courtesy of Kilns and Furnaces Ltd.*

time switch very useful for automatically switching on the kiln in the early hours of the morning while I was soundly asleep and I then finished off the firing using pyrometric cones at around midday, which was my most convenient time. I did find that the firing time varied by as much as half-an-hour either way but after a while I could guess approximately how long the firing was likely to take with that particular kiln to within fifteen to twenty minutes. This represented little more than one cone variation and with the types of clay and glazes I was using this would not have had catastrophic effects had I relied solely on the time switch which had been set to switch off automatically about half-an-hour after the time at which I had estimated the firing would be completed.

The kiln sitter

This is an American device which provides a means of arranging the collapse of a miniature cone to operate a switching device to cut off the electrical supply to the kiln.

As will be seen from Fig. 9 the equipment comprises a metal box containing a heavy-duty mechanical switch from which projects a heavy porcelain tube at the end of which is carried the miniature cone supported across two fixed metal rods. A high-temperature heat-resistant feeler rod lies on the cone and a claw fitted to the feeler rod at the opposite end holds a counterweight in position.

The equipment is set to commence firing by pressing in a self-locking push-button to close the switch. When the required temperature has been reached the cone bends, thus altering the setting of the feeler rod, which results in the claw being lifted thus releasing the weight. In falling, this weight releases with a snap action the heavy-duty switch.

Full instructions are provided and the equipment is easily fitted by drilling a 1-inch hole through the kiln case and brickwork, inserting the ceramic tube and drilling and screwing the metal case to the kiln case with the screws provided. The price is similar to that of an indicating pyrometer.

Fig. 9 The kiln sitter.
Courtesy of Wengers Ltd.

3 Pyroscopes and Temperature Control

Some way of controlling the firing of a kiln is essential to obtain consistently good pottery. Before the intensive study of pyrometric practice, the sense organs were the only means of determining temperatures and kiln firemen estimated the temperature of a kiln by reference to the degree and colour of the glow inside it. The determination of temperature by sight and feel, however, can only be an approximation and it is quite inadequate for modern industrial practices and the modern studio potter.

Pyrometers and pyroscopes

There are basically two methods of controlling a kiln firing: by the use of pyrometers and by the use of pyroscopes (pyroscopes such as Staffordshire cones are often referred to as pyrometric cones). Pyrometers and pyroscopes are, however, often used in conjunction as they measure two completely different functions. Pyrometers measure temperature, pyroscopes measure heat work.

Pyroscopes are indicators made of ceramic mixtures based on silicates. The chemical nature of silicate mixtures is such that they do not have definite melting points but they have a temperature range in which part of the mixture is melted and the remainder is solid. In this temperature range the process of glass formation (vitrification) takes place. When a sufficient degree of vitrification occurs the pyroscope can no longer support itself and bends or collapses, thus giving a visible indication. There are, however, two ways of attaining this result. The first is to heat the pyroscope to a temperature high enough to produce this effect quickly. The second is to heat to a slightly lower temperature but to hold this temperature for a longer time.

Since pyroscopes tend to be of a similar composition to pottery bodies they offer a very good means of controlling the finishing point of a kiln firing. Pottery is correctly fired when the correct degree of vitrification has taken place — as are pyroscopes. If a kiln firing is done slowly this will be reached at a lower temperature than when the firing is done very quickly. Thus the reliance on pyrometers alone to determine the finishing point of a kiln firing can be a little misleading.

Pyrometric cones

These offer possibly the most important and useful way of controlling a kiln firing for the studio potter. They are commonly classified as pyroscopes; Bullers rings and Holdcroft bars fall into the same category.

Suppliers generally offer pyrometric cones in two sizes — 'Standard' cones which are 2½ inches tall and 'Miniature' cones which are 1 inch tall. The cones themselves are of a three-sided conical shape. They are made of carefully controlled mixtures of ceramic materials; these mixtures are so designed as to give a graduated scale of fusing temperatures at approximately 20-degree intervals.

The cones which melt at the lower temperatures contain a higher proportion of fluxes than those melting at the higher temperatures. This melting or fusing temperature is denoted by a number which is stamped into the back of the cone and by reference to the pyrometric cone chart one can obtain an approximate melting-point for each of the different numbers. It is, however, commonly assumed that pyrometric cones will always melt at the temperature indicated in this chart. This is not so. Pyrometric cones melt and collapse not necessarily when a specific temperature has been attained but also when they have been subjected to a certain temperature, or rate of temperature increase, for a certain length of time. It is this time factor which is so important: if one fired a kiln, say, to $1000°C$ in, say, three to four hours, the pottery ware fired in the kiln would not be

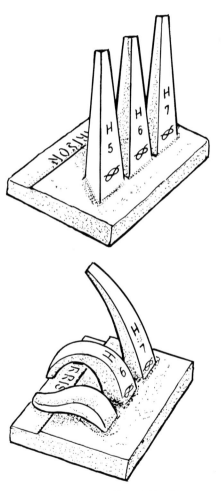

Fig. 10 Cones correctly set (*top*); cones correctly fired to H6 (*bottom*).

fired to the same degree as ware fired to $1000°C$ over a period of eight to ten hours. This, of course, is rather obvious but many potters erroneously believe that because the ware has been fired to its recommended temperature the pottery is bound to be fired correctly.

The important point is that pyrometric cones only collapse when subjected to heat for a certain length of time and if they are fired too rapidly they will not collapse until a temperature is reached which may be considerably above that indicated by the number stamped on the back of them. Similarly, if the cones are fired too slowly then they will probably collapse at a temperature earlier than that indicated by the cone number. In this way pyrometric cones give an indication of the amount of heat work applied to the ware and not merely the temperature to which the ware is subjected. Pyrometers measure temperature; pyroscopes measure heat work. The two are not the same.

It should be noted that other factors can influence the temperature at which pyrometric cones collapse. If they are used in a strongly reducing atmosphere then it is possible for a chemical reaction to take place which results in a hard refractory skin being formed on the outside of the cone. The cone may then stand quite upright and the temperature of the kiln continue to increase considerably beyond the point at which the cone was supposed to have collapsed. It is even possible for this hard skin to be formed and yet for the inside of the cone to melt and run away, with the result that the refractory shell of the cone which may be still standing upright misleads the operator. Sulphur gases can also attack pyrometric cones, resulting in bloating and a grey discoloration which, again, tends to distort the collapsing temperature.

One of the most important considerations in the use of pyrometric cones is the way in which they are mounted. This is generally done by inserting the base of the cones either into special cone holders or into a pad of plastic clay, but regardless of the type of mounting it is important that all the cones be embedded to the same depth. It is necessary for the cones to be placed at a certain angle to the vertical and to ensure this the manufacturer slants the base of the cone so that this inclination is automatically brought about when the cone is stood upright (with its base horizontal).

It is usual to use a series of three cones for each firing, one cone indicating a temperature about 20 degrees below the temperature to which the ware is to be fired, one cone indicating the required temperature, and one cone indicating a temperature some 20 degrees above the required one. In this way the collapse of the lower cone serves as a warning that the temperature is rising to the point at which the second cone will collapse (at which time the kiln should, of course, be switched off). The third cone serves as a guard — as an indication that the ware has not been overfired. An alternative layout sometimes used by the craft potter is to dispense with the 'guard' cone and to use an extra warning cone collapsing at a temperature some 40 degrees below the required temperature of the fire.

It is important to place the cones in some definite order and this is generally done by placing the cones from left to right in order of increasing fusion point so that the cone on the extreme right will be the last to go down. The correct firing of any cone will be indicated when the cone bends over so that its tip bends down and touches the base on which the cone is mounted. This is referred to as the end-point of the cone. If the temperature continues to increase the cone will, of course, collapse still further and eventually melt completely.

There are three main types of pyrometric cones in use: Staffordshire cones manufactured in the UK, Orton cones manufactured in the USA and Seger cones manufactured in Germany. Since Seger were the first in the field the name has become a generic term but this can be misleading for it is a fact that if theoretically the same Staffordshire, Orton and Seger cones are fired together in the kiln they do not collapse exactly together. Thus one cannot change from one cone to another without prior evaluation by simple comparison tests.

Staffordshire cones (having an 'H' prefix to the cone number) incidentally conform to the British Standard (B.S.1041: Part 7: 1964).

Bullers rings

These are another form of pyroscope made from a carefully controlled mixture of ceramic materials. They take the form of a flat ring some 3 inches in diameter, about ¼ inch thick and with a hole in the middle, and are used in conjunction with a Bullers ring gauge.

Bullers rings are placed vertically in a special holder and after firing they will, of course, have contracted considerably with a consequent reduction in diameter. This degree of contraction is measured by placing the ring into the gauge and observing the number indicated on the scale, which is calibrated from zero (zero being the indicated reading of an unfired Bullers ring). The number indicated on the scale is referred to in the Pottery industry as the number of 'pips'. Potters consequently tend to speak of a Bullers ring firing of a certain number of pips. Bullers rings are not commonly used by studio potters, because of the expense of the gauge and the amount of space taken up by the ring during firing. They are, however, very extensively used by the larger industrial concerns because of the uniform rate of contraction over a wide range of temperature. This enables the tunnel kiln fireman to determine the amount of heat work being put into the kiln at any point along its length by the simple expedient of opening up the appropriate spy-hole (these are situated at intervals all the way along the side walls of the tunnel kiln), inserting a poker and 'hooking' the Bullers ring through its centre hole from the car travelling through the kiln immediately opposite the spy-hole. When cool, the ring can be measured in the gauge and, if the reading is substantially different from those previously taken from the same point, corrective action can be taken.

Holdcroft bars

These are another form of pyroscope which take the form of bars of ceramic material of a square cross-section of about ¼ to ½ inch and about 3 inches in length. They are stamped with a number from one to forty, which can be related to a chart graduated from 600—1550°C.

Holdcroft bars are placed horizontally on two supports so that the ends of the bars only are supported. The ceramic mixtures of which they are made begin to melt so that the bars collapse in the middle when the approximate firing temperatures, indicated in the charts, have been reached.

Fig. 11 Holdcroft bars (a) before using (b) after using.

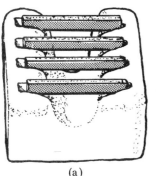

(a)

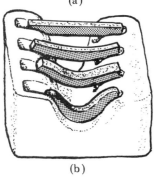

(b)

Fig. 12 Stoneware bowl by Don Rushton fired in an electric kiln to cone 9. The pot is made from Red St Thomas clay with an alumina matt glaze over slip (Cornwall stone glaze).

4 An Introduction to Thermoelectricity

The basic form of pyrometer is a simple temperature-indicating device consisting of a thermocouple and a galvanometer. There are, of course, special ways of adapting this basic instrument to enable it to control the firing temperature or firing cycle to a considerable degree — and these variations will be discussed more fully in the next chapter.

Thermocouples

However, before we can go on to discuss the different types of pyrometers which are available to the craft potter, we should perhaps discuss thermocouples in greater detail for this is the 'working end' of the pyrometer, the end which projects inside the kiln and which generates the current which is measured by the instrument fixed outside the kiln.

If two different metals are drawn into wires and they are joined together at one end, a small electric current is generated when this joint of the two wires is heated. The greater the amount of heat applied to the junction the greater will be the

Fig. 13 Simplified sketches of a thermo-electric pyrometer.

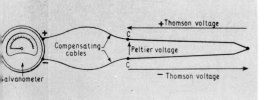

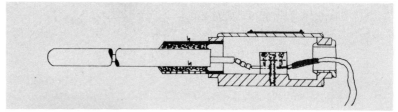

voltage generated in the wires. By measuring this voltage one can, therefore, get some indication of the amount of heat being applied to the junction of the wires. If the junction of the wires is plunged into, say, boiling water, the voltage recorded on the galvanometer (the instrument) can be marked with the temperature 100°C, since this is the boiling-point of water. Similarly, if the end of the thermocouple is plunged into boiling sulphur, the reading on the galvanometer can be calibrated for 444°C, since this is the boiling-point of sulphur. In this way we can calibrate our galvanometer to read degrees of temperature as well as voltage, and if this were done over a range of different temperatures we should then have an instrument which would be capable of measuring temperature. We should have created a thermoelectric pyrometer, to give this instrument its full name. We can see that this is made up of a thermocouple and a galvanometer. The voltage generated by thermocouples is, incidentally, very small, being measured in thousandths of a volt (millivolts) rather than in volts.

It should be noted that there are several different types of thermocouples and the amount of voltage generated at any particular temperature differs with each type. For this reason one cannot generally use one galvanometer and attach to this different types of thermocouples. The metals from which the thermocouple wires are made differ with different types of thermocouples. Some of the more commonly used thermocouples are as follows.

Copper—Constantan
Copper for one wire, Constantan (made of 60 per cent of copper and 40 per cent of nickel) for the other. This can be used for temperatures up to 600°F (315°C).

Nichrome—Constantan
Nichrome (an alloy of 90 per cent of nickel and 10 per cent of chromium) for one wire and Constantan for the other. This can be used for temperatures up to 1600°F (870°C).

Iron—Constantan
Iron for one wire and Constantan for the other. Used for temperatures up to 1600°F (870°C).

Chromel—Alumel
Chromel (a nickel-chromium alloy) for one wire, Alumel (an alloy of nickel, aluminium, manganese and silicon) for the other. Used for temperatures up to 2100°F (1150°C).

Platinum—10 per cent rhodium
An alloy of 10 per cent of rhodium, 90 per cent of platinum for one wire and pure platinum for the other. Used for temperatures up to 2700°F (1480°C).

Platinum—13 per cent rhodium
An alloy of 13 per cent rhodium and 87 per cent of platinum for one wire and pure platinum for the other. Used for temperatures up to 2700°F (1480°C).

Of these, the types normally used in ceramics are the Chromel—Alumel and the platinum-rhodium and platinum types. Platinum is, of course, a very expensive metal and for this reason the thermocouples based on platinum are very much more expensive than the Chromel—Alumel types. It will be seen that temperatures up to 1150°C can be satisfactorily recorded by the use of Chromel—Alumel thermocouples and if one is not going to fire to temperatures higher than this, then for economic considerations, this thermocouple is to be preferred to the platinum type.

The thermocouple wires have to be insulated from one another and this is generally done by passing them through small porcelain tubes. The insulated wires are then immersed in a refractory sheath in the form of a tube closed at one end which serves to protect the thermocouple from certain harmful gases present in the kiln atmosphere. The other end of the sheath terminates in the thermocouple head on which are located the terminals to which the wires carrying the voltage back to the galvanometer are connected.

The voltage generated by the thermocouple is due to two completely different effects known as the Thomson and Peltier effects respectively. In 1834 Peltier discovered that when two different metals are joined together a difference in voltage exists between them and that this varies with the temperature of the junction. Usually when the junction is heated the voltage generated increases proportionally but with certain metals the rate of increase of voltage begins to decrease again at certain temperature ranges. In 1854 Thomson discovered that when a length of metallic wire is heated at one end a difference in voltage between the ends is created. Sometimes the heated end is at a higher voltage than the other but sometimes the reverse is true.

When selecting wires from which to make thermocouples the manufacturers must ensure that the Peltier and Thomson effects complement one another. They must, therefore, choose two wires whose Thomson effects are in opposite directions and vary uniformly with temperature. They must ensure that the voltage

Fig. 14 Typical thermo-couple fitted with compensating cables.

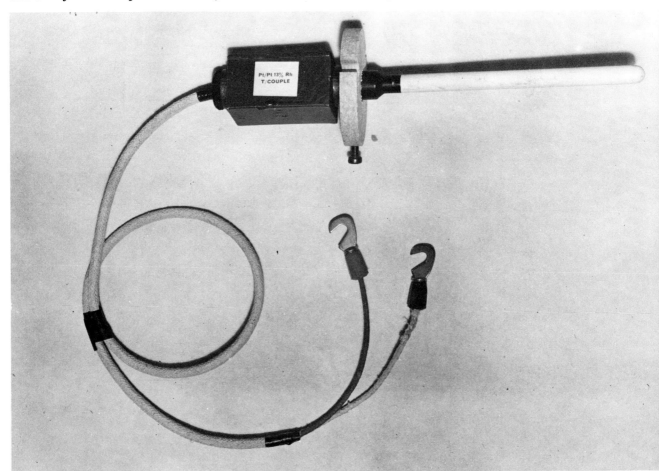

generated by the Peltier effect is such that the wire carrying the negative Thomson voltage must be the positive element as far as the Peltier voltage is concerned. The voltages created by the two different effects will then support one another and will tend to vary uniformly with temperature provided that the cold end of the thermocouple wires is held at a known and constant temperature.

The cold end of the thermocouple is generally referred to as the 'cold junction', the end of the thermocouple projecting into the firing chamber being referred to as the 'hot junction'.

It should always be remembered that the voltage generated by a thermocouple is dependent upon the difference in temperature between the hot and cold junctions and to register temperature accurately it is very important for the cold junction to be kept always at the same known temperature. The reason for this is that the wires which connect the cold junction of the thermocouple to the galvanometer (these wires are referred to as compensating cables) will in themselves generate a small voltage between the cold junction of the thermocouple and the galvanometer. In this case the galvanometer serves to unite the ends of the compensating cables. The Peltier effect of the compensating cables will vary if the temperature of this junction of the cables is allowed to vary. Similarly, any cold junction variation will affect the voltage created still further. Providing that we keep the cold junction and the galvanometer at a constant temperature, the small Peltier voltage generated by the compensating cables via the galvanometer can be corrected by calibrating the latter.

If heat is applied to the thermocouple or compensating wires at some point along their length, the voltages created by this additional source of heat will tend to cancel themselves out, provided that the respective temperatures of the hot and cold junctions are not affected.

5 Temperature-measuring Instruments (Pyrometers)

Temperature-measuring instruments are of different types but the ones generally used by studio potters consist of a thermocouple attached by compensating cables to an instrument which transforms the voltages fed into it from the thermocouple into degrees of temperature which are indicated on a scale. The indicating instrument itself is generally one of two types: either a galvanometer (i.e. a millivoltmeter) or a potentiometer. The standard pyrometer generally has a simple galvanometer as the recording instrument whereas the more sophisticated recording instruments generally have potentiometric systems or a combination of the two.

Potentiometers

The word 'potentiometric' occurs frequently in temperature measurement systems and describes merely the system used inside the recording instrument to measure accurately and to convert into degrees of temperature the very small voltages fed into it from the thermocouple. A potentiometer compares these minute voltages with a precise voltage generated by a battery system inside the instrument, or by mains voltage.

The principle is that the voltage from the thermocouple is amplified and compared to a voltage picked up from a 'slidewire' resistance carried by an indicating pointer or, more usually, a temperature control pointer. Any difference thus devised can be used to either drive the temperature indicating pointer via a servo motor to the appropriate position or switch on or off a contactor or the kiln directly.

In this chapter I will briefly discuss the different types of instruments commonly used by studio and school potters. Each instrument has a different function although some instruments offer the same means of control as others but in a more sophisticated form. Obviously the choice of the most suitable type of instrumentation will depend not only upon the job it has to do but largely also upon personal preference and to a certain

Fig. 15 Stoneware bottle by Don Rushton fired in an electric kiln to cone 9. Made from red St Thomas clay with a wood ash glaze.

degree upon whether the kiln operator can be constantly available or is available only for short periods to attend the kiln. If one has the time to attend to the kiln whenever necessary to change settings, switch off, etc., then one does not really require more than pyrometric cones, an energy regulator (or three-position switch), and perhaps also a standard pyrometer.

The cost of certain instruments, such as the Thermolimit, temperature regulator, controlling pyrometer and programme controller, will vary to some extent depending upon what type of electrical components are already fitted to the kiln. Each of these instruments, for example, must be wired in conjunction with a contactor, the price of which increases with kiln size. Contactors are fitted as a standard fitment to some kilns and are fitted on all kilns which use a Sunvic-type energy regulator.

Most temperature-indicating instruments are of a delicate nature and the manufacturers stipulate that they should be serviced at regular intervals if accuracy and reliability are to be maintained. Furthermore, it is always a wise precaution to carry out the first few firings by relying upon pyrometric cones and to use the instrument solely as a reference — just to ensure that it is functioning correctly. Remember, however, that cone and pyrometer reading comparisons are very approximate and there may be a significant difference between the temperature reading on the pyrometer and that suggested by the cone chart.

Important 'Do's' and 'Don'ts' when installing pyrometers

Don't connect electric mains supply to pyrometer/thermo-couple terminals.

Don't run the compensating cables near or parallel to electric mains as otherwise the compensating cables will have an electric current induced in them from the mains cables, which will result in inaccurate readings on the instrument.

Don't drill holes in the pyrometer case for any purpose whatsoever. If a different mounting is required the pyrometer should be returned to the factory for modification.

Don't open the pyrometer when dust, dirt, fumes or metal dust are in the atmosphere.

Don't use ordinary copper cable for connecting the thermocouple to the pyrometer, as this will not compensate for temperature changes.

Don't shorten or lengthen the cable or thermocouple as the pyrometer has been calibrated for external resistance.

Do get a qualified electrician to install mains operated pyrometers and controllers. There are too many accidents where expensive instruments are ruined or where people have suffered from electric shocks.

Other important points

The temperature inside the kiln is indicated on the pyrometer dial at all times. Do not adjust the instrument to read zero if the kiln is at room temperature.

When pyrometers are being packed for despatch, a connecting wire is always joined between the pyrometer terminals. This 'shunt' wire prevents the indicator needle from swinging about violently if the pyrometer is jolted, and must be removed before the instrument can be used.

Pyrometers must not be positioned where they are subject to radiant heat, draughts or dampness, and the surrounding temperature should not exceed 35°C. They must also be checked with a spirit level to ensure that they have been mounted perfectly level — this is very important.

The standard pyrometer

This consists of a galvanometer fitted with a temperature scale, a thermocouple housed inside a porcelain sheath, and two pieces of compensating cable for connecting the two. All brackets and fixing instructions are normally provided.

Installation is simple — the metal framework of a kiln is often drilled by the manufacturer at a position suitable for the installation of a thermocouple. All that is necessary is to extend the hole through the brickwork (easy: the brickwork is very soft) and push the thermocouple into the hole so that not less than about 1¾ inches is projecting into the firing chamber of the kiln. The galvanometer is connected, by the flanges provided, on to the side or roof of the kiln, and the compensating cables are connected between the terminals of the thermocouple and the two terminals on the instrument, making sure that the red wire is connected to the red terminals and black to black. A screw fitted to the front or just underneath the front of the instrument

Fig. 16 Standard indicating pyrometer.

can then be adjusted to set the instrument reading to the room temperature (i.e. normally about 18°C) or, more precisely, the actual temperature inside the kiln.

The thermolimit

This is sometimes referred to as a Pyrolimit. It consists of the same type of thermocouple as is used for the standard pyrometer and the same compensating cable. The instrument is, however, much more sophisticated.

The instrument is usually of the potentiometric type and carries a temperature scale on a bigger dial (7 inches) than the standard pyrometer (4 inches). In addition to the temperature-indicating pointer (normally black in colour) the instrument also has a further pointer (normally red) which can be manually set to any position on the scale. The black pointer indicates the temperature inside the kiln at all times but when this indicating

Fig. 17 Thermolimit (Limitstat) controller coupled with a process timer. The two-position soak off switch below the controller allows the instrument either to cut off the kiln when preset temperature is reached, or to actuate the timer to provide a timed soaking facility before switching off completely. *By courtesy of Industrial Pyrometer Company.*

pointer reaches the setting at which the red pointer has been manually fixed the instrument is automatically cut off, which in turn cuts off the electricity supply to the kiln, and firing therefore stops.

The controlling pyrometer

This is very similar in design to the Thermolimit but incorporates extra circuits which enable the instrument to act as a thermostat, if necessary, to maintain the kiln at one particular temperature, which is preset by a manual setting of the red pointer referred to in the description of the Thermolimit.

The instrument is fitted with a two-position switch which is referred to as a 'soak—off' switch. When the switch is set to its 'soak' setting the instrument will act as a thermostat once the temperature-indicating pointer reaches the setting of the manually fixed red pointer and the supply to the kiln elements is therefore switched on and cut off to regulate the temperature at the temperature indicated by the red pointer. If, however, the switch is set to the 'off' position the instrument will function like a Thermolimit and automatically switch off the kiln when the black indicating pointer reaches the red one.

It is occasionally desirable to keep the ware at a certain temperature for a short period of time and the controlling pyrometer would obviously enable this to be done when the 'soak—off' switch is set at its 'soak' setting. If the kiln is at its preset temperature and needs to be switched off, all that is necessary is to move the switch to the 'off' setting when the kiln will switch off automatically. Moving the switch to the 'off' setting before the temperature of the kiln has reached the temperature preset by the red pointer will not, of course, result in the kiln switching itself off — it will only do this when the black pointer reaches the setting of the red one.

Fig. 18 Controlling pyrometer enabling firing temperature to be preset by means of knurled adjuster and the actual temperature to be checked by pressing soak-read switch to 'read' facility. If left in the 'soak' position the instrument will allow the kiln to reach pre-set temperature and hold that temperature indefinitely until manual shut-off.
By courtesy of Industrial Pyrometer Company.

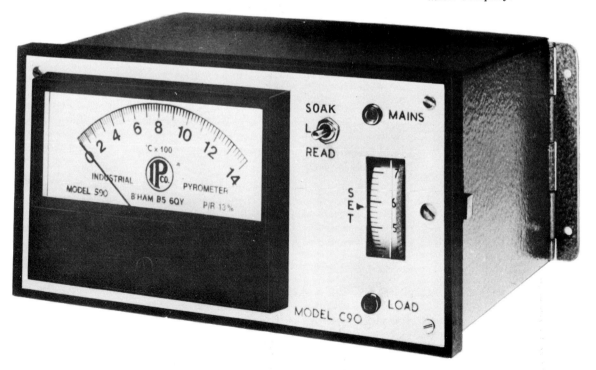

Fig. 19 Temperature regulator. When set at 'stat' the instrument causes the kiln to soak at the preset temperature. If set at 'Limit' the kiln will cut off when the temperature is reached.
By courtesy of Industrial Pyrometer Company.

The temperature regulator

The thermocouple section is identical with those used for the other pyrometric instruments, but the instrument is not fitted with a temperature-indicating pointer and is therefore much more robust in its ability to withstand knocks and jolts.

The face of the instrument is fitted with a control knob which can be rotated within a scale graduated up to 1400°C. When the kiln is switched on, no matter how quickly the temperature rises it will never exceed the temperature indicated on the scale by the control knob. The temperature regulator therefore functions exactly like a thermostat fitted into the oven circuit of an electric cooker and, like a cooker thermostat, is fitted with a relay to switch the electricity supply on and off.

Two indicating lights are often fitted to the instrument: one of these lights up only when the temperature regulator is allowing current to pass to the elements, the other light being constantly illuminated whilst the instrument is in operation.

I have never been able to understand why this instrument is not much more popular than it is. Perhaps the suppliers are at fault for not advertising it more or perhaps we are all so accustomed to using instruments having moving pointers to indicate temperature continuously that this disadvantage of the temperature regulator is allowed to overshadow completely its compensating advantages. As there is not the delicate mechanism involved in the operation of a movable pointer, the instrument is considerably more robust than other types of pyrometers. It enables the kiln operator to maintain the kiln easily at any temperature until it is switched off and it is possible to approximate the temperature of the kiln, if necessary, by moving the knob setting and 'searching' until a setting is reached at which one light on the instrument begins to switch on and off alternately. The price, too, is very competitive.

The programme controller

This instrument is supplied with aluminium templates or cams which are marked with time and temperature co-ordinates. It is therefore easily possible to work out a suitable firing cycle within the capabilities of the kiln and plot this on one of the aluminium cams (drawing a continuous line on the cam very much as one would draw the performance line on a graph), to denote the required rate of temperature increase, maximum temperature, and rate of cooling, etc. The cam is then cut to the contour denoted by the line drawn upon it, and the cam template fitted to the instrument.

The instrument is fitted with a motor which can be switched on and off by means of a switch. When the motor is switched on, the spindle upon which the cam is fitted is caused to rotate very

Fig. 20 A programme controller.

slowly (one revolution per twenty-four hours or so), thus turning the cam with it. As the cam very slowly turns, it deflects a guide (called the cam follower) which is in constant contact with the edge of the cam and as the cam follower itself is connected to a pointer on the temperature scale of the instrument, a deflexion of the cam follower causes a deflexion of the instrument pointer.

This pointer is a 'regulating' pointer but there is also another pointer which denotes the actual temperature inside the kiln; but provided the firing cycle indicated by the shape of the cam is within the capabilities of the kiln the two pointers will move in unison up and down the scale when the kiln is firing. The actual temperature inside the kiln, incidentally, is never allowed to exceed the temperature indicated by the regulating pointer, owing to a thermostat control which would automatically be brought into operation.

It will therefore be seen that the shape of the cam controls the rate of heating or cooling of the kiln and thus it is possible to pre-plan any required firing cycle and to use the instrument to put this planned cycle into practice, the instrument being controlled in accordance with the programme denoted by the shape of the cam. Naturally the cam must be set and tightened in a position which causes the indicating instrument to read room temperature (or the temperature inside the kiln if this is different from room temperature) before the motor is switched on and the kiln firing started.

Note that the cam will only be driven by the instrument motor while the motor switch is in its 'on' position; if the motor is switched off while the kiln is firing, the temperature inside the kiln (which will be indicated on the instrument) will remain constant and will not alter unless the motor is switched on again, which would start the cam rotating.

If the cam is rotated until the instrument registers, say, 1100°C, and the kiln switched on but the motor switch left in the 'off' position, the kiln will increase its temperature at the quickest possible rate until it reaches 1100°C. At this point the kiln temperature will be kept constant until switched off manually or until the instrument motor switch is switched on.

Limit switch
A switching device is incorporated into the instrument which can

Fig. 21 14″ high jug by Michael Hawkins fired in an electric kiln to 1275°C. Made in St Thomas body with iron slip decoration.

be manually set to switch off the instrument and the kiln automatically at any desired temperature. An arrow is printed on the face of the instrument and the instrument automatically switches off when the limit switch lever rotates to a position opposite the arrow.

The lever itself is fitted to the spindle (arbor) upon which the cam is fitted and if, say, one wished the kiln to cut off automatically once a temperature of $1100°$ C had been reached after following a certain firing cycle, the procedure would be as follows.

Fit the cam on to the cam arbor and then rotate the cam until the reading on the instrument shows $1100°$ C. Hold the cam firmly in position and move the limit switch lever until this is opposite the arrow. Tighten the knurled knob on the cam arbor to clamp the limit switch lever firmly into position relative to the cam. When the cam is now rotated back into its starting position the limit switch lever will, of course, move back with it and when the kiln is switched on, and also the motor switch, the cam and limit switch lever will be driven around the scale, the limit switch lever reaching the cut-out arrow when the temperature inside the kiln is $1100°$ C.

These instruments will control the complete firing cycle and this would be particularly useful, for example, when attempting to produce kiln load after kiln load of pieces of the same colour, for the programme controller will ensure that successive firings are very similar to each other and thus a matching colour can be obtained from each firing.

As programme controllers will do virtually everything required in kiln firing they are very sophisticated instruments and are, consequently, the most expensive instruments normally used by studio potters.

6 Basic Effects of Heat on Clay

With the exception of some terracottas and a few stoneware clays most of the clays used by potters are mixtures of different types of clay with other materials mixed in to give desirable properties. For example, most white and ivory earthenware clays are made from blends of different ball clays, china clays, flint and Cornish stone, all of which are mixed together, in liquid form, in carefully controlled amounts. The mixture is then sieved and passed over powerful magnets before being passed to the filter presses, where surplus water is removed to convert the clay from its liquid state to a plastic condition. This plastic clay is then passed through a pug mill where the clay is thoroughly sliced and mixed to give it a very homogeneous consistency.

Vitrification and porosity

Potters speak of some clays as being more refractory than others; by this, of course, they mean that the firing temperature or maturing range is higher for certain clays than others — for example, stoneware bodies which have to be fired at temperatures of about 1250—1300°C are more refractory than earthenware ones which fire at 1100—1150°C. Potters also speak of 'vitrification' and 'porosity', which are terms used to describe the degree of water retentivity of the body after firing. A vitrified body is one that is dense and non-porous, or nearly so, i.e. its porosity is low. The porosity of a body generally decreases as it is fired to higher temperatures.

A body is correctly fired when it has been fired to its

maximum degree of vitrification without deforming or has been fired to a temperature which has enabled the body to develop a sufficient coefficient of contraction to enable glazes to be used without crazing (more about this later). The temperature or, more correctly, the range of temperatures at which this stage is reached varies from one type of body to another and is referred to as the firing range, maturing range or vitrification point of the clay. Some clays, e.g. stoneware, will be almost completely vitrified when this point has been reached, others will possess an appreciable degree of porosity — such as the earthenware and terracotta types.

Each of the constituents of prepared pottery clays plays a different role. The ball clays are generally introduced to make the body plastic and to give it good workability. China clays are generally introduced to add whiteness to the body and are always appreciably more refractory than ball clays. Flint, as we shall see later, supplies silica and is introduced mainly to develop craze-resistance, and stone serves as the flux which melts and holds the other particles together. When the clay has been fired it should not be considered as one homogeneous mass but more as a mixture of different materials suspended in a fluid which has become solid on cooling to hold all the particles firmly in position. Other materials are very frequently used in bodies, for example, felspar or nepheline syenite is often used as a substitute for Cornish stone, and quartz or finely ground sand is sometimes used as a substitute for flint.

Pottery should always be dry before being fired. This is a golden rule. If damp pottery is placed into the kiln there is a great risk of its cracking or literally exploding during the firing operation, and bits would be scattered over all adjacent pottery pieces, probably damaging them. Thick pieces of pottery take longer to dry than thin pieces and they also take longer to fire. If you place thick and thin pieces of pottery into the same kiln the kiln would have to be fired more slowly than would be the case if one were firing thin pieces only.

When clay is fired it undergoes several complex changes and, even though it is dry when being placed into the kiln, a considerable amount of water vapour will be driven off during the firing operation. This arises from the chemically combined water present in the clay crystal and cannot be removed by mere drying. All clays, of course, shrink as they are being dried and they shrink still further during the firing operation. This degree of shrinkage varies from clay to clay but is generally higher in those bodies which have the higher firing temperatures. The more clay present in the body the greater will be the degree of shrinkage.

The importance of silica

Silica is possibly the most important material used in ceramics — it is indeed sometimes regarded as the basis of the pottery industry and it is fortunate for the potter that the majority of the earth's crust contains supplies of silica in one form or another. Flint pebbles found in the chalky strata of parts of southern England are traditionally used by the British potter to introduce silica into the body recipe after the pebbles have been calcined (i.e. burned) and crushed and ground to a powder. In other parts of Europe, and in America, quartz or sand is used for the same purpose. Silica also occurs abundantly in volcanic rocks and consequently also in clays, the decomposition product of volcanic rocks, and in sandstone.

As far as the potter is concerned the most important characteristic of silica is its behaviour when heated. Just as silica can be located in so many different materials so does the silica crystal itself occur in several different forms or modifications. When silica is heated some of it changes from one form to another only to revert to the original form when it is subsequently cooled. Other modifications of silica change permanently to another form and this new form remains when the silica is cooled.

Modifications of silica

The most important crystal modifications of silica are as follows:

α (alpha) quartz	$\rightarrow$ β (beta) quartz
α (alpha) tridymite	$\rightarrow$ β (beta) tridymite
α (alpha) cristobalite	$\rightarrow$ β (beta) cristobalite

Of these the alpha and beta quartz and the alpha and beta cristobalite modifications are of particular concern. Whenever

Fig. 22 Graph showing thermal
expansion of silica materials.

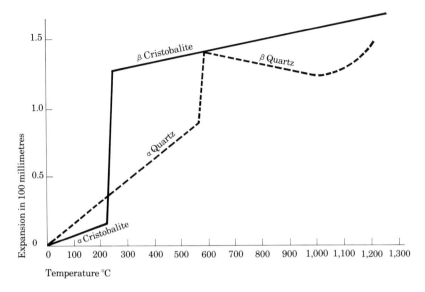

these silica forms change from one modification to another under the influence of heat, an expansion takes place; similarly when the silica is subsequently cooled and beta quartz, for example, reverts to its original form of alpha quartz, a contraction of the silica mass takes place.

Let us now look at this behaviour in more detail. When silica is heated it gradually expands until a temperature of approximately 225°C is reached, when it suddenly expands very considerably as the alpha cristobalite content changes to beta cristobalite, which of course has the same chemical composition but a larger volume. As heating is continued another sudden expansion occurs at a temperature of approximately 573°C, when alpha quartz changes to beta quartz.

However, as heating continues other forms of silica begin to change into beta cristobalite, this conversion progressing with increasing rapidity as the temperature is raised higher. If silica is heated above 1200°C for example, most of it is converted into beta cristobalite. Thus the higher the temperature to which a pottery clay or body is fired, the more cristobalite is developed. This is a very important phenomenon.

As silica is cooled it gradually contracts until a temperature of approximately 573°C is reached, at which point the beta quartz content reverts to its original alpha quartz form accompanied by a sudden contraction. As the silica is cooled still further the point at which beta cristobalite changes back to alpha cristobalite is reached when the temperature drops to approximately 225°C. This beta to alpha cristobalite change causes another sudden volume contraction.

These sudden expansions at certain temperatures when the silica is heated and the sudden contractions at the same temperatures when it is cooled occur every time the silica, or a body containing silica, is fired. They therefore occur during glost firings as well as biscuit ones and if heating or cooling of the pottery is proceeding too quickly the stresses set up by the above silica 'inversions' can, and often do, result in cracks right through the pottery causing the fault known as 'dunting'.

The formation of an appreciable amount of cristobalite renders pottery clays and bodies craze-proof. This is because the beta to alpha cristobalite change as the glost-fired ware is being cooled suddenly shrinks the biscuit ware, causing the glaze covering it to be placed in a state of compression. The most common cause of glaze crazing is not firing the ware to a sufficiently high temperature to produce enough cristobalite in the body. (An exception is porcelain and bone china where excessive firing can cause some of the silica to be dissolved in the body thus producing low-expansion silicates which make crazing worse.)

Stages in biscuit firing

1.   Water smoking
This covers the period from the beginning of the firing up to a temperature of about 150°C. During this period any remaining mechanically held water present in the clay is boiled away. Removal occurs in two ways: firstly, the body continues to contract until each particle touches its neighbour and, secondly, water is removed from between the particles.

2.   Dehydration period
This covers an approximate temperature range of from 150°C up to 600°C. The chemically combined water present in the clay mostly comes away from the body between about 200°C and 460—600°C, but traces are still present up to 900°C. During this

period of time the amount of steam given off from the ware will be about fifty times the interior volume of the kiln and this must be allowed to escape easily from the kiln. If the kiln is heated too quickly from the commencement of firing up to the end of the dehydration period, then steam formed inside the body may not be able to get to the surface quickly enough and may build up to such a pressure that the pottery is blown apart. Firing should therefore be at a fairly slow rate over this temperature range.

3. Oxidation period

This is at 400—1100°C, when most of the carbon present in the clay ware burns away. If this oxidation of the carbon content is not done completely the result may be the formation of what is referred to as a black core inside the body. This can sometimes be seen on building bricks and insufficient oxidation can also result in small black holes being formed on the surface of pottery or problems with subsequent crawling or blistering of glazes.

Incidentally, by 800°C the clay is as porous as a sponge as it has now lost all of its chemically held water and most of the carbon without any readjustment of the other ingredients. At this stage the body is, in fact, lighter in weight than it was when first placed into the kiln and it is extremely porous. If the tip of the tongue is touched against the pottery the tongue will stick because of the suction caused by the biscuit absorbing moisture from the tongue. This phenomenon is used by experienced industrial potters to give a very rough guide as to whether the biscuit ware has been fired to a high enough temperature. If the biscuit is too porous it has not been fired hard enough, if too vitreous it has been overfired.

4. Vitrification period

This covers a temperature range from about 900°C up to the firing range of the clay. Thus, with the craft technique of low biscuit/high glost firing, the vitrification period may take place predominately during the glaze firing. During this period the fluxes present in the body now begin to react with the clays and tend to soften and as the temperature is increased they begin to melt more and more until eventually, if the temperature were taken beyond the vitrification point of the body, gases would be

given off which would lead to bloating or blistering. When this happens the fluxes in the body would be literally boiling. Bloating is, however, often caused by insufficient volatiles being burned away during the oxidation and vitrification periods or by firing too quickly (which amounts to the same thing). Under such circumstances excess escaping gases during the time at which the body is almost vitreous and its surface sealed by molten glaze can swell or blow bubbles in the structure of the pot much as a child blows bubble-gum.

Indeed, if haze builds up in the kiln during the later stages of firing it is advisable to slow down the firing speed or to temporarily remove the bung to clear the kiln.

Fig. 23 Porcelain bowl by Michael Hawkins fired in an electric kiln to 1280°C.

49

7 Basic Effects of Heat on Glazes

Glazes are suspensions in water of materials which will subsequently melt together to form a glass-like material.

Matching of glazes

Glazes have to be 'matched' to the body to which they are applied if good craze-resistance is to be obtained: by this we mean that the rate of expansion and contraction of the glaze must be similar to that of the body otherwise one will obviously crack away from the other if the fired pot is suddenly heated or cooled. The rate of expansion of a glaze depends upon the quantity and rate of expansion of each material used in its composition. Various materials have very different rates and by a careful selection process it is possible, within limits, to design a glaze to have a specific rate of expansion and contraction. If the rate of expansion of the body is known, a glaze can therefore be calculated to suit it and this glaze would then be said to be 'matched' to the body. In actual fact the glaze is designed so as to have a slightly lower coefficient of expansion than the body upon which it is to be used so that during the cooling of the glaze it contracts a little less than the body which therefore 'squeezes' it, i.e. the contraction of the body puts the glaze into a slight amount of compression. This then gives the glaze a built-in resistance against crazing.

Eutectics

Some very strange things can happen when materials are heated,

and glaze constituents are no exception. Silica, for example, which is a constituent of nearly all glazes, has a melting point of 1713°C and is therefore a very refractory (i.e. heat-resisting) material. However, when this is mixed with other materials and melted in the kiln, it combines with the other materials to form new compounds which together have a much lower melting-point — very often lower than the melting-points of any of the materials in the original mixture. This formation of 'eutectics' (i.e. mixtures which have a melting-temperature lower than that of any of their constituents) is a frequent phenomenon.

Fig. 24 China painting kiln designed for firing enamel colours and lustres. This kiln automatically cuts off at the preset temperature.
By courtesy of Potclays Ltd.

When a glaze is heated, the materials from which it is made begin to combine together well before the glaze becomes completely molten. The glaze itself gradually melts and becomes increasingly more molten as heating is continued, until eventually it becomes so fluid that it runs almost like water. When the glaze is cooled it becomes progressively more viscous until, at a temperature of approximately 800—600°C, depending upon the type of glaze, it becomes rigid and ceases to flow.

It would not be strictly true to refer to the glaze as now being a solid. Solids have definite melting points: lead, for example, suddenly melts at a temperature of 327°C, copper melts at 1084°C, and once the temperature drops below their melting-points these materials become solid again. Glazes, like glasses, are known as supercooled liquids which are solid at normal temperatures — they do not have a definite melting-point but gradually soften over a wide range of temperature.

Buffer layer

As the glaze becomes more and more molten it increasingly attacks the body to which it is applied. This reaction between the body and the glaze is very important for it results in a layer which is part glaze and part body, which we call the 'buffer layer' and which helps to fix the glaze firmly to the body. Instead of having a definite layer of glaze upon a definite body — rather like a sheet of water upon a block of aluminium, we have a layer of glaze which merges with a buffer layer of part glaze part body which merges with the body. A good buffer layer helps to anchor the glaze and thus helps to prevent the glaze cracking away, as happens in crazing or peeling.

If the biscuit ware has not been properly fired so that excess gases are given off during the glost firing, these gases can dislodge the glaze film and rupture it. When this happens the glaze may roll back to leave a bare patch — the fault known as crawling. Grease, dust, or dirt on the biscuit ware can cause the same fault.

Bubbles and craters in glaze

During the heating of a glazed article gases escape not only from the body but obviously also from the glaze itself as this decomposes under the influence of heat. When the glaze begins to melt, the escape of these gases becomes increasingly difficult until the gases eventually have to bubble their way through the molten glaze. The speed with which they do this varies from glaze to glaze and depends upon the thickness and fluidity of the glaze layer, but when they eventually do reach the surface they burst and this results in the formation of small craters. The purpose of subsequent heating of the glaze is to enable it to become just sufficiently fluid for it to flow and fill in these craters. If the glost firing is done very rapidly the gas bubbles can be trapped inside the glaze as there is not sufficient time for them to escape through the molten glaze before the kiln is switched off and the glaze becomes solid again. Furthermore, because the glaze would not become sufficiently fluid to allow the craters to be filled in, the glaze would have a pinholed appearance. To achieve a nice smooth glaze surface, free of bubbles and blemishes, it is therefore often necessary to fire the kiln comparatively slowly just before it has reached the recommended firing temperature for the glaze being used, or alternatively to hold the kiln at its firing temperature for half an hour or so.

Stresses and stress release

While the glaze is molten some of the constituents are being vaporized and if this were allowed to continue unnecessarily the glossy glazes would become very dull and lack shine. As the glaze cools towards the point at which it becomes a solid mass this rate of vaporization decreases considerably. To obtain a good glossy glaze the kiln should therefore be cooled fairly quickly down to about 750°C, at which temperature most glazes will be rigid. Any stresses or strains created in the glaze by this rapid rate of cooling will be easily absorbed, for the glaze is molten and any stresses will just flow away. However, as the glaze becomes increasingly more rigid it becomes a very different story; the glaze is now able to crack — and will do so if stresses and strains are caused by cooling too quickly. It is therefore best to fix an arbitrary point of 750°C and to cool as quickly as possible down to this point followed by a much slower rate of cooling.

Fig. 25 Bottle, 28″ tall, by Michael Hawkins fired in an electric kiln to 1275°C and made from a Pyropot body with iron slip decoration and celadon glaze.

Effects of cooling

Another fault known as 'devitrification' can be caused by cooling the glaze too slowly while it is molten. This fault often results in a transparent glaze taking on a milky appearance. There are other causes, but slow cooling is a common one.

With matt and opaque glazes a very rapid cooling is never necessary and in fact with opaque glazes it may hinder the development of the correct amount of opacity.

Once the temperature drops below 700°C care must be taken to ensure that the rate of cooling is slow enough to prevent the ware from cracking. There are two particularly dangerous temperature ranges — at about 575°C and at about 225°C. At these points, for technical reasons discussed in the previous chapter, the silica present in the body undergoes a sudden contraction as it is being cooled, with the result that the body and the glaze layer fixed to it suddenly contract. If all of the body and the glaze covering it reached these temperature points at the same time, and thus shrank at the same time, no problems would occur but this ideal state of affairs is never reached in practice. While one part of the pot may be at one of these critical temperature points, another part of the same pot may well be at a temperature 10, 20, 30 or even more degrees different. During the cooling operation the inside of the pot is, for example, usually hotter than the outside; similarly, during the cooling operation, the foot of a pot resting on the bat is usually hotter than the top of the same pot standing in free air, owing to the high amount of heat retained by the bat. These temperature differences inevitably produce strains which are so magnified by the sudden shrinkage of the pot when part of it reaches the critical temperature points mentioned above that cracking often takes place. These cracks, due to heat stresses, are known as dunts and usually penetrate right through the pot, thus making it fit only for the scrap heap.

To prevent this cracking taking place we must therefore allow the pot to absorb these stresses over as long a period of time as possible and this can only be done by cooling slowly when the temperature of the kiln approaches 575°C and again when the kiln temperature approaches 225°C.

8 Difference in Technique between Craft and Industrial Potters

Pottery ware is normally processed in two firing stages, the first firing of the clay ware which is termed the 'biscuit' fire and the subsequent fire of the glazed ware which is termed the 'glost' fire.

Earthenware, terracottas, and other porous clays

There is a considerable difference in firing technique between craft and industrial potters. Studio or craft potters invariably fire the biscuit ware to a temperature just high enough to make the clay hard and of good porosity so that a good film of glaze is picked up during the dipping operation. This is subsequently followed by a glost firing to a higher temperature than that of the biscuit fire.

Industrial potters, on the other hand, invariably fire their clay ware to a temperature higher than that of the glazed ware. Clays, like glazes, have a range of temperature to which they must be fired if satisfactory results are to be obtained. Let us take a specific example, such as an earthenware or terracotta clay having a firing range of 1100—1150°C. Craft potters would generally fire this clay to a temperature of about 900—1050°C and then follow this with a glost firing to 1100°C or higher, which would serve to develop both the body and the glaze at the same time. Industrial potters, however, would fire these clays at a biscuit firing of 1100°C or higher, which would serve to develop the clay, and would then follow this with a glost fire using a glaze that matures at a lower temperature, say 1050°C.

The industrial technique definitely tends to give better results in that there is less loss from the glaze firing than there is with the craft pottery technique. The only disadvantage is that after the biscuit firing the biscuit ware is comparatively vitreous (non-porous) and it is consequently much more difficult to pick up a good layer of glaze during the dipping operation. For this reason industrial concerns always go to great lengths to make sure that the glaze being used in the dipping tubs is of exactly the right consistency to ensure a satisfactory pick-up of glaze, and for really vitreous bodies the industrial potters use spraying techniques to apply the glaze coat, which overcomes the glazing problems associated with a non-porous body. Alternatively, binders or flocculents can be added to the glaze to increase glaze pick-up. An addition of half to a few teaspoonfuls of saturated calcium chloride solution to each gallon of glaze for example will enable relatively vitreous pieces to be dipped quite easily, although a small addition (1 per cent) of bentonite to the glaze should also be made to prevent the glaze from settling too quickly.

There are other advantages to be gained from the industrial practice of firing the biscuit fire higher than that of the glost. During the subsequent glost fire the body is comparatively inert since it has already been fired in the biscuit fire to a temperature higher than anything reached during the glost fire. With the craft pottery technique, once the temperature of the glost fire surpasses that of the biscuit, the body itself becomes much more reactive and gases are once again given off by the body which now have to bubble their way through the film of glaze covering it. This may result in pinholes or other glaze blemishes. This does not happen to anything like the same extent with the industrial technique as it minimises the tendency of the glaze to blemish.

Another advantage is that since the body will have been fired to its maturing point on the first fire any warping or distortion that is likely to take place will take place during this firing and not during the subsequent glost firing. If it was required to glaze a thin, pencil-like object, the industrial potter would do this by firing the clay to its maturing temperature during the biscuit fire, and during this time the object would be left lying flat on a bat or other suitable support to prevent distortion. During the glost fire, which would be at a lower temperature, the same object could be supported merely on its two ends with comparatively little risk of distortion. The craft potter, trying to fire the same piece, would find that it would distort very considerably during the glost fire unless it was supported at points other than at its ends, which would result in marks being left on the glost surface.

The craft potter forgoes all these advantages of the industrial technique in order that he may get a high porosity on the biscuit ware which enables him to apply the glaze very easily.

It should always be remembered that, provided one is using satisfactory glazes and bodies, the temperature to which the body is fired controls the degree of craze-resistance developed by the pottery ware. It is true that crazing difficulties can sometimes be overcome by firing the glost firing a little higher than was done with previous glost firings and it is generally assumed that the increased craze-resistance arises directly as a result of reactions in the glaze following the extra heat to which it has been subjected. This is not strictly true: the increased craze-resistance is also due to the increased amount of heat applied to the body via the glaze layer.

In addition to the two-fire method (biscuit and glost), pottery can also be fired by a one-fire process. This involves applying glaze to clay ware and then firing this once to a temperature which is high enough to develop both the body and the glaze at the same time.

Stoneware and porcelain

Where stoneware and porcelain are concerned — and the special qualities of these bodies are being appreciated by more and more potters — the pots would be so vitreous after being fired to the full maturing range of the body that the craft potter would be faced with difficult application problems if he wished to apply glaze by a dipping process. With these bodies the craft potter therefore invariably follows the low biscuit/high glost firing technique.

Biscuit firing is therefore carried out at about $1000°C$ after which the glaze can easily be applied to the very porous biscuit. The glaze is then fired at the appropriate temperature to suit the glaze in the range $1220-1300°C$ or sometimes even a little higher in the case of porcelain.

The quality and texture of stoneware and porcelain glazes are, incidentally, often enhanced by the gases which inevitably bubble through from the biscuit ware and also by the reactions which take place between the glaze and the decomposing body. Indeed much stoneware pottery owes its success and appeal to the glaze effects brought about by a high-temperature glost firing.

Bone china

To obtain the characteristic translucency of bone china it must be fired to the point at which the body almost melts. It is therefore always biscuit fired to around 1240°C (some use a biscuit firing to about 1200°C followed by a long soak until the 1240°C cone goes down) and an earthenware type glaze is then applied and fired to about 1060°C.

To prevent the ware from distorting or collapsing during the biscuit firing it has to be placed on special setters, buried in calcined alumina, or supported with rugged bone china clay props. Obviously, glazed ware could not be treated in this way, which is why the high biscuit/low glaze firing technique has to be used.

9 Kiln Furniture and Loading the Kiln

Loading a kiln for firing, often referred to as 'kiln placing', can be an art in itself; with practice you can acquire an eye for using almost all of the available space. Experienced potters can fit a large amount of ware into a small space while leaving adequate room for air circulation.

Kiln furniture: shelves and props

With the studio electric kiln the pottery is placed on shelves made up of from one to four kiln bats depending upon the size of the firing chamber. If elements are fitted into the hearth (base) of the kiln the pottery should not be placed directly on the hearth but on a kiln shelf placed ½—1 inch clear of the base. This prevents possible damage to elements if a pot should break and in addition allows a more even heat distribution throughout the kiln. If the pots to be placed are comparatively small in size, then several shelves may be needed and these are supported one above the other by kiln props of which there are different types, the most popular ones being castellated props, tubular props and cast props. Castellated props are basically tubular but have interlocking turrets on them — rather like the battlements of a medieval castle. Tubular props are refractory cylindrical tubes available in various lengths. Cast props are usually solid cylinders which have a dome at one end and a recess at the other — so that they can be interlocked. A number of small props, say 1 inch or 1½ inches in height, will obviously make it possible to alter the distance between shelves with ease, but a series of props one above the other obviously do not give such a stable assembly as one large prop of the same height. Flat circular discs of a greater diameter than the kiln props are often placed between a kiln bat and the prop immediately below it as these help to spread the load on the shelf and reduce the risk of shelf collapse — particularly where there are two or more bats per shelf and one prop, or column of props, is supporting two bats.

An important point is that each bat should be supported at three points as this prevents the 'rocking' which might occur if the bat was supported at each of its four corners — a three-legged chair or stool will never rock but a four-legged one might. The supports should be arranged in similar positions for each succeeding shelf so that the total weight of the complete set of kiln furniture acts downwards through continuous columns.

During biscuit firing the pottery shrinks considerably and if warping is to be avoided this shrinking action should not be arrested by any irregularity on the kiln shelf. The best way to assist this shrinkage is to place a thin layer of silver sand (silica sand) over the shelves as each particle of sand will act like a

Fig. 26 Kiln furniture and placing accessories used for glazed ware.
A: pin crank. B: collar. C: cast prop.
D: castellated prop. E: tubular props.
F: kiln bat. G: stilts. H: spurs.
I: saddles. J: tile crank. K: tile bat.
L: tile 'dots'.

ball-bearing in assisting the contraction of the pot. During glost firing, however, a layer of silica sand on the kiln shelves can be a nuisance due to sand particles sticking to glazed pots resulting in rough spots on the fired ware. However, during glost firing some buffer layer between the pot and the kiln shelf is desirable in case any particles of glaze have been left on the pot base which would cause the pot to stick firmly to the kiln shelf. The ideal material for putting on the shelves for glost firing purposes is a mixture of alumina and china clay or zircon and china clay mixed with water and painted on the shelves in the form of a wash so that it adheres quite firmly. Many companies sell a specially prepared mixture known as bat wash, which is quite cheap.

If the same kiln is being used for alternate biscuit and glost firings it is best not to use silica sand at all but to rely solely upon the bat wash used for glost firings, as the risk of contamination of the glazed pots from particles of silica sand is considerable.

In any case the kiln furniture should be checked after each firing and any loose particles of bat wash lightly brushed away. Spots of glaze sticking to the shelves must be chipped or ground away and the area painted over with a new layer of wash. Cracked kiln bats should either be discarded or, if the crack is a very fine one, supported by a prop placed underneath the crack. This regular check is important and should always be done.

Kiln shelves and props are usually made from sillimanite or a mixture of refractory materials similar to sillimanite. These materials are very refractory and will easily withstand stoneware temperatures although if one requires the kiln bats to withstand temperatures up to $1300°C$ without warping then it is best to select bats either ¾ or 1 inch thick; ½ inch thick kiln shelves are very popular but these are best reserved for temperatures below $1200°C$. Kiln furniture made from silicon carbide (carborundum) can also be obtained. There is little doubt that silicon carbide kiln furniture is generally superior to the sillimanite types — it is stronger and has better heat conductivity for example — but it is extremely expensive and for this reason is seldom used.

Some potters make their own kiln bats from refractory clays such as Potclays Crank mixture or fireclay and grog mixtures but these are never as strong as industrially manufactured bats of similar thickness formed under immense pressure. Home-made kiln furniture is often prone to premature or sudden failure.

Fig. 27 Glazed pots supported inside the kiln.

Biscuit kiln placing

Loading a kiln for a biscuit fire is simpler than loading one for the glost as all that is really necessary is to place the pots inside the kiln with the object of getting as many pots as possible into the smallest possible space. The firing of a kiln costs money and waste of space is, therefore, money thrown away. With the smaller kilns one does not have a very great deal of free space in which to design the best layout of the pots in order to obtain a high packing density but with the larger kilns one can often rearrange the pots placed on kiln shelves to obtain a more tightly packed arrangement. Some potters find it helpful to simulate the space available in the kiln by marking a suitable working surface with a full scale plan of each kiln shelf. While the kiln is in use pots can be arranged into their respective firing positions so that when the kiln is ready for repacking the pots can be quickly transferred to their pre-planned position in the kiln.

When clay pots are fired they progressively shrink and will have a tendency to warp if the design of the pot does not give it adequate support and if the biscuit firing is taken up to the full maturing temperature of the clay, as is sometimes done with earthenware and terracotta clays.

In the biscuit fire, with all clays except bone china, it is permissible to place one pot inside another if this is at all possible. Thus a small bowl can be placed inside a larger one. Do not, however, make the error of packing too many pots inside another as the largest pot may give way during the firing — one should remember that for a short time during the biscuit fire the pots become weaker than they were when placed into the kiln. Only experience can determine the amount of weight that a certain pot is capable of holding. Clay pots can be placed upside down or on their side if this is helpful in obtaining tighter packing inside the kiln and if there is no increased risk of warping. Fire lidded pots can keep their lids on to ensure equal shrinkage and subsequent fit.

Large heavy pieces may need shrinkage platforms under them to prevent warpage. These are smooth slabs of clay made from the same clay as the pot and which shrink to the same extent as the pot. A thin layer of bat wash or silica sand should be placed between the shrinkage platform and the shelf to enable the clay platform to shrink easily without sticking to the shelf.

Closed-in shapes such as vases or teapots are comparatively easy to fire because their compact forms have a structural resistance to warping. Cups and bowls are more liable to warp and identical pairs of these are often 'boxed' together, i.e. one on top of another (rim to rim) and stuck together by a gum such as gum arabic, which burns away during the firing. Thin pieces, of course, will warp much more easily than thick ones.

When loading ware for either biscuit or glaze firing, remember to leave a gap of at least 1 inch between the pot and the nearest element so as to prevent scorch marks or excess shrinkage appearing on one side of the pot.

Finally, the cones should be placed into position and checks made to ensure that they are in a position directly in line with the spy-hole in the kiln door. Close the kiln door and you are ready to begin firing.

A most important point is that any clay ware placed into a kiln must be DRY. Damp ware is liable to crack or literally explode (thus damaging other pots), as a result of steam pressure built up inside it when firing begins.

Glost kiln (loading)

Much more care must be taken with loading a kiln for the glost
fire than for the biscuit fire as the glaze coating will stick the pots
together if they are allowed to touch. Similarly, should any
glaze adhere to the underside or foot of a pot that is placed
directly onto a shelf, the pot will be firmly stuck there after
firing.

Many pots *are* placed flat but the glaze is always removed from
the base of the pot beforehand either by use of a wax resist, by
scraping or, more usually, by using a sponge or a damp piece of
felt. If you want to glaze the underside of a pot or if you want
additional reassurance that no sticking is likely to occur then
several different kinds of support can be used on which the pots
can be placed to keep them clear of the kiln shelf. In Fig. 26 is
an illustration of some of the more popular types of supporting
items such as stilts, saddles, spurs, etc. These are quite
inexpensive and it is false economy to continue to use them after
several fires as the sharp edges of these items tend to become
blunt after repeated firings. A new stilt, for example, will hardly
leave a blemish on the base of a pot even if this is covered with a
thin layer of glaze, whereas a stilt which has been in use for
several firings may have the points removed and may have to be
broken away from the base of the pot after firing, leaving
unsightly marks which will have to be rubbed down.

Stilts and small saddles are particularly useful in the firing of
glazed earthenware, terracotta, buff and bone china wares to
support the pots clear of the kiln shelf, and a further advantage
of using these is that the air circulation under the pots helps to
reduce the temperature variation between the top and bottom of
the pottery article. This will help to prevent the occurrence of
cracking or dunting.

Have you ever noticed the three marks on the underside of a
saucer between the rim and the foot ring? These are the three
points at which the saucer was supported on special 'cranks'
during the glost fire in an industrial kiln. These cranks are
refractory racks into which identical plates or saucers can be very
tightly placed, and they are very extensively used throughout the
ceramic industry. Pin cranks, as they are called, can only be used
for glazed ware if the biscuit ware has been fired to a higher

temperature than the glost as otherwise the plates or saucers placed inside the crank would warp during the glost firing. They can, therefore, be used to advantage with glazed earthenware, terracotta or bone china wares but not with stoneware or porcelain. Stilts, spurs and saddles also are unsuitable for use with stoneware and (especially) porcelain, since such wares would tend to squat and deform over them if the pottery was fired to its normal maturing temperature. Consequently it is usual to leave stoneware and porcelain items unglazed at their base so that they can be set down flat upon the kiln shelf for glost firings.

No matter how careful you are when placing the pots into the kiln you are likely to dislodge a few specks of dirt or bat wash and for this reason the top shelf should be placed first, followed by the shelves underneath. If any dirt is dislodged it will therefore fall downwards on to an empty shelf and not into or on to glazed ware. This procedure cannot, of course, be followed with top-loading kilns nor is it easily possible where the variety of pot size demands the use of half shelves.

Do make certain that any bat wash painted on the kiln shelves is quite dry before beginning to place ware into the kiln as it is surprising how damp bat wash gets on to the fingers and then on to the glazed pots. Incidentally, it is not usually necessary to give a complete coating of bat wash to the shelves after every firing but merely to 'touch up' those areas from which traces of glaze deposited during the previous firing have been removed. Periodically it is a good idea to rub away the layer of bat wash with a flat grinding stone (not the Carborundum type) and then carefully to brush off the shelves, subsequently giving them a new coat of wash.

Some points to remember

Craft potters usually biscuit fire to around $1000°C$ and then fire the glaze to a higher temperature (except with bone china). During glost firing the pottery body will remain relatively inert until the temperature reaches that of the biscuit firing after which point further reaction and shrinkage takes place.

This further shrinkage is particularly marked with stoneware and porcelain and one has to check that pots are not set in the kiln in a position which allows them to shrink down onto supporting refractories, e.g. cone holders or the feet of certain types of kiln props.

If any kiln bats are cracked they should either be discarded or broken into two pieces for use as half bats, etc. If the crack is a minor one it is usually possible to make use of the bat with very little risk of failure, provided that a prop is used to support the bat immediately under the cracked area.

Kiln furniture must be quite dry before being subjected to the normal firing schedule as otherwise it may be caused to crack by escaping steam. Sometimes, fine cracks may be caused in a kiln bat due to damage during handling or transit. These fine cracks which may not be easily visible but which could be a source of bat failure can often be more easily detected by sprinkling a powder such as alumina over the surface of the bat and then sharply tapping the bat in the centre. This causes the powder to move away from any crack in the bat, revealing the crack as a line in the pot.

When loading ware for either biscuit or glost firing leave a gap of at least 1 inch between the pot and the nearest element. Failure to do this may result in one side of the pot being scorched.

When placing glazed ware into the kiln hold the pieces firmly; trying to hold pieces delicately with thumb and finger is much more likely to result in the glaze film becoming damaged — unless, of course, the pots are very small. If any is knocked away during the placing process then apply some more, either touched on with a finger or soft brush, followed by rubbing smooth when dry.

It is best to avoid as much as possible placing differently coloured glazed pots in the same firing. If this cannot be avoided then try to keep white and highly pigmented glazes, for instance black, as far away from each other as possible as volatilization of glaze from one pot can influence the colour of its neighbour to a very noticeable degree. For example, a pink tinge on a tin glazed pot may result if it is placed near to one containing chrome.

Don't forget the pyrometric cones and do ensure that when they collapse they will not fall against a pot which has been placed too close to them — a point easy to overlook.

10 Biscuit Firing

We have seen that terracottas, earthenware and other clays, which are porous when fired to maturing temperature, would be biscuit fired in the industry to the full maturing temperature of the clay. Craft potters, however, would generally biscuit fire at the same temperature as is used for stoneware and porcelain, i.e. at around 1000°C in order to obtain good porosity to facilitate adequate and easy glaze pick-up.

Clay firing temperatures

It should be remembered that the fired porosity of stoneware, earthenware and terracotta clays will be different after a firing to the same temperature. Clays of different compositions but similar firing range may also be quite different in porosity after firing. Potclays 1141 white and 1135 red clays are both suitable for 1080—1150°C, but the red clay will always be more vitreous at any temperature. The biscuiting temperature of a mixed load should therefore be carefully considered since there will be a variation in glaze pick-up.

Most craft potters biscuit fire around 1000°C and glaze fire higher, but the important point to remember is that the firing temperature of the clay must be reached at some point in the pottery process and with porous bodies this may be attained either during the biscuit or the glost firing. With stoneware and porcelain fire to about 900—1100°C, as firing these clays to the full maturing temperature will render the ware too vitreous to glaze easily. If Staffordshire cones are being used in the firing, the ones selected should obviously be those corresponding to the required firing temperature.

During the period of time that the pottery is being fired several very complicated chemical reactions take place and the firing schedule should be such that these reactions can take place unhindered. For all practical purposes, however, these reactions can be grouped into two phases: the first phase being the formation of steam and the second phase being the burning away of all the organic (carbonaceous) material present in the clay. As was explained in a previous chapter, most of the steam which is formed in the clay is generated over the first $100-300°C$ or so and firing should consequently be done comparatively slowly over this range. Most of the burning away of organic materials takes place immediately afterwards and continues up to about $1100°C$.

The most important of these two phases is the first one — the liberation of steam, as the rate of temperature increase of kilns is usually not so rapid that all the carbonaceous matter cannot be burned away. I know of many potters who merely take care over the first hour or so after the kiln is switched on and then allow the kiln to continue its temperature rise at a medium or high rate with apparently no ill effects. A lot does depend upon the kiln, the amount of ware inside the kiln and particularly the thickness of the ware being fired.

We will, however, assume that the pots to be fired are not thicker than ½ inch: this should cover 90 per cent of the pottery produced by school and studio potters. If the pottery is thicker than this then the rate of temperature increase of the kiln must be slower in order to allow the heat generated inside the kiln really to soak into the ware.

Firing

After all your clay ware has been safely placed into the kiln and the kiln door closed you are ready to commence firing.

Heating up
First of all the vent plug should be removed and perhaps the spy-hole left open as well. If an energy regulator is fitted to the kiln this should be set at a fairly low setting; if the kiln is fitted

merely with a three-position (low, medium, high) switch, then the switch should be set at its 'low' position.

The object of this procedure is to ensure that during the early stages of firing the water vapour chemically held inside the clay, which is converted into steam, is allowed to escape from the kiln very easily. The rate of temperature increase should be fairly slow and certainly not greater than about 100 degrees per hour for the thinner pieces of pottery. The thicker pieces of pottery will demand a temperature increase considerably slower than this — perhaps as low as 50—70 degrees per hour.

The kiln will now gradually increase its temperature and large amounts of steam (which may not be seen) will be escaping from the vent-hole and spy-hole, of the kiln. After about two to four hours the kiln can be switched to its 'medium' setting of the three-position rotary switch or, if an energy regulator is fitted instead of this, the regulator can be turned up to a reading of about '60' on the scale. At this point the temperature should be in the region of 200—350°C.

At the same time the vent plug may be placed firmly in position at the top of the kiln. If, however, there is a large amount of organic matter in the clay (this is generally so with stonewares and fireclays) or if the pots are very tightly packed inside the kiln, it will be better to delay putting the vent plug in position for a further hour or so. Alternatively, some potters place the vent plug across the hole for a short while so that the hole is not properly sealed. In any event kilns are not airtight and gases will escape even when the vent plug is firmly in position.

The actual brickwork lining the interior of the kiln will begin to glow a red colour at a temperature of about 600°C and at about 650—700°C will be glowing very noticeably. At this point the kiln will probably have been on medium setting for about two to four hours and it can now be switched to its high setting to finish off the firing for the terracotta and earthenware types of clay. For stoneware clays it is normally best to allow the kiln to remain for a further hour or so at its medium setting before switching to the high one, since many of these clays contain a comparatively high amount of carbon — particularly those with a fireclay content.

If the vent is still open the plug must now be placed into

position as heat would needlessly be wasted and a marked temperature gradient would be generated inside the kiln.

After switching to the high setting of the three-position switch or the 100 per cent setting of the energy regulator the kiln will now begin to increase temperature at its maximum speed. If experience shows that this rate of temperature increase is too rapid, then it may be best on future occasions to switch only to the 90 per cent setting of the regulator or less.

A firing to $1000°C$ should normally take about ten hours i.e. $100°C$ per hour on average. This may, of course, mean that heating would be faster than this average on 'high' settings to compensate for a slower rate in the earlier stages.

The kiln interior by now will be glowing brightly and after a further two or three hours the temperature will probably be in the region of $800-1000°C$. If a pyrometer is fitted you will be able to determine the point at which you should start looking into the kiln to check the pyrometric cones. This procedure should normally begin when the reading on the pyrometer gives an indication of some 30 degrees or so before the first cone is due to collapse. If a pyrometer is not fitted then one must rely upon glancing into the kiln through the spy-hole about every half-an-hour or so until the first cone begins to collapse. When this happens look into the kiln every ten minutes and switch the kiln off the moment the cone to which the ware is being fired has collapsed.

Cooling down

The rate at which kilns cool varies from model to model and naturally also depends upon the temperature and amount of ware and shelves inside the kiln. It is best to leave the kiln as it is until the interior temperature drops to about $100-150°C$, when the door can be opened in stages.

Inspection

When the pots are taken from the kiln examine them closely. If any of them appear to be a greyish colour then there is probably still some organic matter inside them, in which case you will know that the temperature increase of future biscuit firings must be retarded by leaving the kiln on its medium setting for a longer period of time. If the pots are extensively cracked then one possible cause is that steam pressure built up inside the pot has had to rupture the pot to burst its way out. If this is the case then the kiln must be allowed to remain at its 'low' setting for a longer period of time on future firings. Clay cracking, however, can be caused by a very 'short' (i.e. not very plastic) clay or by working with the clay in too dry a condition, by not drying the pots evenly, or by drying them too quickly. In these cases the cracks will be present in the clay ware when placed into the kiln, although they may be so fine as not to be visible to the unaided eye; the biscuit firing will most certainly open them up, however.

Summary

Most kiln manufacturers recommend an average rate of temperature increase of about 100° per hour although the first two or three hours firing time may be slower than this. Comparatively thin pieces of pottery — say of a maximum thickness of ¼—½ inch — can be fired quite safely with this schedule, but very thick pieces — say thicker than ¾ inch — will need a slower firing rate, particularly in the early stages.

It is common practice to select a set firing cycle based upon experience of the first few firings and then to keep to this for all future firings for a similar type of ware. A typical firing schedule could well be as follows: 'three hours on low with the vent plug out followed by switching to medium for two hours followed by inserting the vent plug and switching to high'.

Schools particularly may have a problem in not having sufficient time to complete a firing. If this is so it is quite permissible with most kilns to leave the kiln at its low setting overnight as the kiln temperature will not rise above 400—500°C at this setting. Then the following morning the kiln can be switched directly to its medium or high setting and the firing thus completed later in the afternoon.

As kiln manufacturers generally provide a graph with each kiln showing how quickly the kiln temperature will rise at various settings of the energy regulator or rotary switch, it is possible to calculate roughly how long a firing to a certain temperature under a set firing procedure will take.

11 Glost Firing

If glazed terracotta or earthenware is to be fired then it should be fired to a temperature slightly below that at which the biscuit ware was fired if the industrial practice is being followed, or to a higher temperature than the biscuit ware was fired if the usual studio pottery technique is followed. The temperature to which the ware should be fired is, of course, the firing temperature recommended for the particular glaze being used and the glost firing should always be taken to this recommended temperature — no matter at what temperature the biscuit firing was done.

If stoneware or porcelain is being fired then the glaze firing will be done at a temperature of 1250—1300°C, the clay ware having been fired to a biscuit temperature of 900—1100°C.

Firing procedure

Switch the kiln on to its low setting for one hour just to drive away surplus moisture retained by the biscuit ware as a result of glaze application. This may not be necessary if the dipped ware is allowed to dry thoroughly before placing the ware into the kiln. Many potters also leave the vent plug out during this initial firing period to allow steam to escape more easily but it is usually not necessary, particularly if the dipped ware has been dried out.

Switch the kiln on to the medium setting of the rotary switch, or to a setting of about 50—70 on the energy regulator if fitted, and leave on this setting for two hours or so before switching to its highest setting. Here again, many people dispense with the medium position altogether during the glost firing and aim to get the kiln to its highest setting at the earliest possible time. Much depends upon the maximum heating rate of the kiln and upon the type of glaze being used (raw glazes need slower firing than fritted ones). An average over the complete firing of 100—120°C per hour would be reasonable but faster or slower rates are in order provided that no cracking, crazing, crawling or dunting is experienced. The vent plug should be firmly in position during this period and should remain in position until the kiln is switched off.

As the kiln temperature approaches the required glaze firing temperature, gas bubbles will still be escaping through the glaze layer and thus forming craters in the glaze, and if the firing has proceeded very rapidly up to this stage then there may not be sufficient time for these craters to heal over before the kiln is switched off. The best thing to do is to slow down the rate of temperature increase over the last 50—100 degrees or so of the kiln firing if the kiln has been fired at a faster rate than about 100 degrees per hour, and then to observe the results when the kiln has cooled. If the glaze surface is pin-holed or has an 'eggshell' or 'orange peel' effect or contains a large number of bubbles then reduce the rate of temperature increase during the latter stages of the next firing, or 'soak' the kiln for half an hour or so before switching off. This can be done by turning down the setting of the energy regulator or switching the three-position switch to the medium setting at frequent intervals. Do not remove the vent plug to slow down the rate of temperature increase as this will result in a wide temperature variation inside the kiln.

Once-firing

With this technique — which is sometimes referred to as 'raw glazing' (although this term more properly refers to a glaze made up of 'natural' or 'raw' materials rather than synthetic or fritted ones) — the leather-hard clay ware is glazed using a glaze containing an appreciable addition of clay or bentonite (to allow the glaze shrinkage to conform to the pot shrinkage). Since the glaze firing develops with both the clay and the glaze at the same time it is necessary to follow a compromise of the careful temperature rise needed for biscuit firings with the slow climax or soaking period needed for glost firings.

Successful results depend largely upon a good match of glaze and body with a careful firing. The whiter clays can be once-fired much more easily than buff or red-burning ones.

Small kilns

Reference should be made here to the very small pottery kilns having internal dimensions of approximately 6 X 6 X 6 inches or less. Most of these kilns were originally designed as testing kilns and as such have been invaluable to many ceramic laboratories both in industry and in educational establishments. They are, however, also used by craft potters for the firing of small items or for the firing of ceramic beads for jewellery, etc. Such kilns will usually heat up very quickly when set at their maximum setting — many of them are capable of attaining 1300°C in as little as three and a half to four hours, for example — so to obtain a good glaze finish it is usually necessary to keep the kiln at a comparatively low setting of the energy regulator which is usually a standard fitment.

Cooling the kiln

When firing of the pottery kiln is completed — as will be indicated by the collapse of the correct cones or the correct firing temperature indicated on the pyrometer — the kiln should be switched off. The speed with which kilns then cool varies widely from one type of kiln to the next. Some kilns cool down too slowly to allow the best results to be obtained from glossy glazes and if this is so the cooling cycle may be speeded up by partial or complete removal of the vent plug (if fitted) but the plug must be fully replaced when the temperature of the kiln has dropped to 750°C.

On the other hand some kilns (small ones or low thermal mass types) cool down too quickly for best results to be obtained from matt or certain crystalline glazes. Under these circumstances it may be necessary to 'fire down' i.e. to switch to a much lower setting instead of switching off the kiln so that the kiln cools more slowly over the first 300°C or so below glaze firing temperature. With a mixed batch of glazes — and always when trying out a new kiln — switch off, leave to cool normally with the vent plug in position and then check the results which generally will be quite satisfactory.

Below 750°C the kiln should be allowed to cool normally (with the vent plug in position) until the temperature drops to about 130°C when, if necessary, the cooling rate can be speeded up again by removing the vent plug or progressively opening the kiln door. The door must *not* be flung open as the cold air suddenly entering the kiln may crack the pots or the kiln shelves: open the door in stages — no more than merely releasing the tight seal between the door and the kiln at first followed by opening the door slightly ajar about fifteen minutes later.

Opening up the kiln after a glost firing to observe the results is one of the thrills of the potter's craft and all too frequently impatience is allowed to get the upper hand. There may be good reasons for speeding up the cooling rate from switching off the kiln down to a temperature of about 750°C if the kiln is of a type that naturally cools very slowly over this range, but from 750°C down to room temperature it is best to allow the kiln to cool as slowly as possible — and particularly while the kiln temperature passes the quartz and cristobalite inversion points. I have mentioned that cooling can be speeded up once the temperature has dropped to 130°C, but this is mentioned because many teachers particularly have to conform to a tight time-schedule and it is essential to remove the fired pottery from the kiln at the earliest possible time.

I should perhaps end this chapter by saying that you will generally be able to obtain very satisfactory results with your kiln merely by switching it on at a medium to high setting of the rotary switch or energy regulator, switching it off again when the required temperature has been reached, and opening up the kiln when it has cooled approximately to room temperature. There must be very many potters who fire their kilns with complete satisfaction by following this basic, very simple procedure. Indeed when kilns are fired with the aid of an instrument such as a Thermolimit, temperature regulator, or controlling pyrometer they are normally fired and cooled at a more or less constant rate. You will, however, generally be able to obtain even better results if you appreciate what is happening inside your kiln at any particular time and can act as the catalyst in adjusting the kiln to make the firing cycle more appropriate to the immediate requirements.

12 Reduction

Effect of reduction

A reduction atmosphere results when the kiln atmosphere becomes overloaded with carbon. When this happens sufficient oxygen cannot be obtained by the materials being burned to ensure their complete combustion. Under this condition the constituents of clays and glazes 'fight' amongst themselves, thereby forcing some of them to give up part of their oxygen content. For example, green copper oxide loses some of its oxygen and becomes red copper oxide. Similarly red iron oxide becomes black iron oxide. The red colour produced by the reduction of copper oxide results in the beautiful *sang-de-boeuf* or ox-blood colour whereas black iron oxide formed by the reduction of red iron oxide can produce a greyish green colour known as celadon.

Effect on elements

So much has been said in the past about the great danger to electric kiln elements that it is commonly assumed that reduction either cannot be done, or cannot be done economically in an electric kiln. This is not necessarily so provided that certain basic pointers are observed. I have mentioned in an earlier chapter that the Kanthal elements used in most electric kilns, and for all those kilns fired over a temperature of 1150°C, are covered with a protective oxide layer when in use. This oxide layer is greyish in colour and serves to seal off the element metal itself from harmful gases in the kiln atmosphere which would otherwise seriously attack the metal thus reducing element life considerably. During a reduction firing this protective grey coating begins to reduce in thickness until eventually it disappears. However, usually two or three firings are necessary for this coating to be removed to such an extent that the element metal is showing through. This protective coating is restored to the elements after a normal firing — and by 'normal' we refer to the usual oxidising fire. It is therefore possible to create a reduction atmosphere in an electric kiln without excessively rapid element failure provided that the protective coating on the elements is not allowed to deteriorate seriously. In practice, after a reduction firing you should observe the element coating to see if the film is becoming thin. If there is any evidence of this, an oxidising fire must be carried out to restore the coating to its usual thickness. It may take one, two or three oxidising firings to restore the coating.

If the reduction atmosphere is not a very powerful one it may indeed be possible to carry out two or three reduction firings before an oxidising fire is necessary. Reduction firings, then, can be carried out with electric kilns with reasonable economy provided that these elementary precautions are observed. Element life will certainly be reduced even if these precautions are observed but nowhere near as quickly as would be the case if reduction firings were carried out haphazardly. It is impossible to give an opinion on how much element life will be reduced by reduction firings. So much depends upon the length of the firing and the degree of atmosphere reduction, etc., as to make it impossible to give an assessment. It is even impossible to give an estimated firing life for elements under normal oxidising conditions — I have known elements to fail after a few months' use yet I have a friend in Tunbridge Wells who has been firing two or three times per week for eight years without ever needing a replacement element.

Even the element wire manufacturers cannot give any guidance on this point but the general feeling is that under conditions of reduction one can expect about half the element life obtained under oxidising conditions — if that is anything to go by. However, the characteristic qualities of many reduced pots often enable the potter to demand higher prices than would otherwise be the case and this factor alone may more than compensate for the reduced element life.

So much for the practicability of reduction atmospheres, but how do we produce them?

Formation of reduction atmosphere

This can be done by putting into the kiln sufficient highly organic material to burn up most of the oxygen in the kiln atmosphere, thus leaving little or none at all for the pottery ware. By the term 'highly organic' we refer to any material which has a high carbon content and which demands a lot of oxygen to burn it away completely into carbon monoxide or carbon dioxide gas. Charcoal obviously has a very high carbon content but there are also several other materials that potters could use. Some people use moth balls but although these produce a reduction atmosphere very efficiently, the gases given off are very toxic and tend to make the kiln very dirty inside resulting in a slight glazing effect on the brickwork and elements. Others use a drip-fed oil system or a gas burner inserted or built into the kiln. Local reduction can also be obtained on the pot by adding one per cent to four per cent very finely ground silicon carbide to a suitable alkaline glaze; one per cent copper oxide or carbonate added to the glaze will then provide a good copper red under normal firing conditions.

The glaze constituents are in their most reactive state and thus most susceptible to the effects of a reduction atmosphere when the glaze is at a high temperature and in a molten condition. Sufficient reduction can usually be obtained by introducing the carbonaceous material as top temperature is reached, continuing additions until the kiln is switched off and has cooled to about 750°C. This may all sound so very simple but in actual practice it is not very easy to introduce carbon into the kiln at these high temperatures. Dropping a lump of charcoal into the kiln could easily damage the pots.

Many potters overcome this problem by placing a suitable receptacle at a suitable position in the kiln to catch the pieces of charcoal. Charcoal can be introduced either through the spy-hole or through the vent-hole at the top or back of the kiln. To maintain a reduction atmosphere inside the kiln it is necessary to replace the vent plug or the spy-hole plug as soon as the charcoal has been safely lowered in. Every twenty minutes or so add more charcoal to the kiln.

Usually the use of reduction is reserved for high-fired work with stoneware so as to obtain the special colours mentioned above. At low temperatures, and particularly when low-solubility or other lead-containing glazes are being used, a reduction atmosphere should be avoided, for the lead content of the glaze will be reduced, forming an unpleasant greyish black discoloration in the glaze.

Lustre glazes can be made by loading the glaze with a very high metal content and then using a reduction atmosphere to form a metallic lustre on the surface of the glaze.

The characteristic colours produced in glazes by reduced forms of certain materials cannot be obtained by adding these materials already in reduced form to a glaze followed by a normal oxidising firing. Red copper oxide cannot, for example, be added to a glaze followed by a normal firing in an attempt to achieve the characteristic copper red colour obtained in a reduction firing. During the normal firing the red copper oxide would be oxidised and one would obtain the usual copper-green-coloured glaze (or turquoise-blue in an alkaline frit glaze).

13 Decoration Firing

Hardening-on fire

In the industry, biscuit ware decorated with underglaze colours (using dilute gum arabic or similar media) is generally fired to around 600—650°C to fix the colours firmly into position. This fire — referred to as the 'hardening-on' fire — also serves to burn away the media and other volatiles to leave the decorated areas with a porosity similar to the rest of the pot so that glaze is picked up evenly over the whole pot surface during dipping. Craft potters, however, generally dispense with this firing operation or decorate the clay ware so that the biscuit firing carries out the hardening-on operation. If a separate hardening-on fire is needed it is therefore sufficient to fire at about 100—120°C per hour up to about 400°C with the bung out then to switch to a higher setting, replacing the bung and continuing the fire until the kiln is switched off at 650°C. The firing would take about four to six hours but could be faster than this under suitable circumstances. Too fast firing will cause the colour to lift away from the surface or to bubble.

Enamel firing

The practice of decorating glost ware with transfers (decals) or by brush decoration using on-glaze enamels, liquid gold or other lustres, is widespread in the industry. It is also a popular hobby (china painting) in many countries (especially the USA)and is now growing rapidly in the UK. In china painting, bone china ware is preferably used since its value, character and soft earthenware type glaze lends itself so well to the process. Porcelain and other ware types are also widely used but all true porcelains have a high-fired glaze and some may be so high fired that the enamel colours lack shine where they are thinly applied unless the ware is fired higher (with some risk of firing away or affecting the colour) or more flux is mixed into the enamel. The medias used are very varied and may be simple turpentine/fat oil mixtures, clove oil, lavender oil, anise turpens, aniseed oil, synthetic resins, emulsions or a variety of others.

Since finished (glost) ware is being decorated and since the enamel decoration invariably needs to be reproduced so exactly, care is needed to ensure adequate ventilation of the kiln whilst the media are being burned away and to switch off the kiln at the right moment.

As with all firings, the ware should be dry when put into the kiln. The kiln can then be fired on low for about three hours and then on to medium or whatever combination is necessary to provide a firing rate of about 100–120°C per hour with the vent plug out up to about 500°C. The vent plug is then inserted and the kiln switched to high or left on medium to take the temperature up to a point normally in the range 720–750°C when it is switched off and left to cool. Thus a firing might be expected to take six or seven hours.

This procedure will generally give good results but with experience it becomes possible to vary the firing cut off point to more closely suit the colours being fired. Colours of identical firing requirements can then be applied and fired together followed by another group at a slightly lower temperature and the process repeated as necessary until the required design is completed with the lowest temperature firing. This is invariably done with prestige or high quality pieces but with others one enamel firing may suffice.

With experience it is also easy to increase the firing speed. The vent plug can usually be inserted earlier than the 500°C mark and particularly with some of the emulsified medias where the products of combustion are largely gone at 200–250°C. All media give off a characteristic smell when being fired and if this odour from the kiln ceases before the 500°C point then the vent plug can generally be safely inserted. In industry, incidentally, enamels are often fired quite rapidly and, particularly with low thermal mass kilns (which cool very quickly), three firings or more per day from the same kiln are often carried out.

Too fast firing whilst combustion products are being burned away can lead to frizzled or bubbled colours. Leaving the vent plug out too long does no harm but wastes heat and therefore electricity. It also allows a wide temperature variance inside the kiln (which incidentally is not remedied until some little while after the plug is inserted — it may take $100°C$ or more temperature rise before the kiln becomes temperature stable).

Fig. 28 Typical craft pottery kiln.
Courtesy of Potclays Ltd.

Appendix 1

Colour of fire/temperature relationships

Temp. °C	Approx. Staffs. cone no.	Orton cone no.	Colour of fire	Effect on clay	Type of ware and glazes
225	—	—	No visible colour, i.e. 'black heat'	Alpha to beta cristobalite inversion	
575	—	—		Alpha to beta quartz inversion	
600	022	021			
750	016	017	Dull red		Firing temperature for on-glaze enamels (china paints)
830	013	014			
850		013			
875	011	012	Cherry red		Raku and lustre glazes
920	09	09		Most of organic matter burnt away by this time	
960	07	08	Cherry red/orange		Low firing lead glazes sometimes opacified with tin oxide (majolica)
1000	05	06		Terracottas mature	Porous biscuit earthenware
1020	04	05			
1100	1	03	Orange changing to yellow/orange	Earthenware matures	Terracottas, industrial earthenware, biscuit earthenware and china glost
1150	3A	1			
1200	6	6	Distinct yellow orange	Terracottas melt. Increasing beta cristobalite formation	Semi-porcelain
1250	8	7			Bone china biscuit, salt glazes, stoneware and some porcelain
1280	9	9	Yellow		
1300	10	10			
1350	12	13	Intense yellow-white		Porcelain
1460	16	16			

The data given for Staffordshire cones is based on a temperature rise of 240°C per hour; while that for Orton cones is based on a rise of 150°C.

Appendix 2

Safety recommendations for electrically-operated kilns

Statutory requirements

Electrically operated kilns are subject to the Electricity (Factories' Acts) Special Regulations 1908 and 1944 in the same way as any other electrical apparatus. Reference should be made to these regulations for fuller details, but briefly their requirements are detailed below. Additionally, it should be borne in mind that electrical equipment in schools may be subject to regulations laid down by the Local Education Authority.

Summary of recommendations

1. All kilns must be provided with convenient means of isolation for the electrical supply and be protected against overloadings and short circuits. The means of protection may be a circuit-breaker or fuses of suitable capacity for the circuit concerned. All conductors (i.e. wiring to the kiln and its control panel) should be sufficiently protected against damage, for example by enclosure in screwed metal conduit, or by the use of wire-armoured cable, or mineral-insulated metal-sheet cable. All metal works other than conductors must be properly earthed.

2. For all types of kilns, the control panels or cubicles must be arranged to prevent access to live conductors, except by authorised persons. Such persons would be electricians who, for the purpose of fault-finding or testing, may occasionally require a panel to be live and accessible.

3. Doors on control panels should be securely fixed and other openable parts of the enclosure must be securely bolted on. It should not be necessary to open any door, or remove any cover exposing live conductors, in order to make any adjustment normally carried out by the operator.

4. Kiln doors must be incapable of being opened by the operator while power is being fed to the kiln. Thus, the door must be filled with either an approved fail-safe, positively operated switch (sometimes used on small kilns switching below 15 amps), or by an interlock system of trapped key-type, or similar. The main point is that electricity supply must be broken by the switch or interlock (and not by the holding coil on the relay), so that the kiln door cannot be opened without the switch actuating.

5. For detailed information regarding the electrical arrangement of particular kilns, users should get in touch with the kiln manufacturer or the Local Electricity Board, District Office. If electrical problems arise with regard to compliance with the Electricity (Factories Act) Special Regulations 1908 and 1944, HM Electrical Inspector of Factories should be consulted.

Additional precautions

Location

Kilns should be positioned so that there is free air movement all round the kiln and the kiln should be at least six inches away from any wall. The ceiling or roof should be a minimum of 2 ft 6 in above the kiln, but if either the walls or the ceiling are of combustible materials, then these dimensions would need to be increased. If there are such ceilings, these should be protected by a heat-resistant board fixed with a two inch air gap between the board and the ceiling in the area immediately above the kiln. It is recommended that the nature of walls and ceilings be determined and if you are in any doubt, contact the local Fire Officer and/or the kiln manufacturer for advice.

Kilns should ideally be located in rooms separate from main class-rooms. They should be sited so as to permit access for servicing, but if this is not feasible then it should be possible to move them in order to permit such access.

Ventilation

The kiln room should be adequately ventilated by means of sufficient windows that open, or extractor fans, so that there is no build up of excess fumes. Although it is not mandatory at present, it is our opinion that a canopy to duct heat and fumes away from the kiln and directly to the outside atmosphere will, in due course, be demanded. This is now mandatory for oil and gas fired kilns. It is recommended therefore that kilns be sited with a view to provision of such equipment at a later date.

Element changing

This should be carried out by competent electricians only. Installation of electrically operated temperature controllers should also only be undertaken by qualified electricians.

Protective cages

These are recommended where kilns are in open plan areas and/or where children can easily come into contact with the kiln. Such cgaes prevent access to the kiln except through a door which can be kept safely locked. We feel that provision of such cages is essential in situations where there are physically or mentally handicapped persons undergoing instruction. It should be remembered that when the inside of a kiln is at high temperature the exterior may also be at a temperature of up to about 240°C (usually around 140°C) and this may cause burning to a handicapped person, who might not be able to pull away in time if there were accidental contact.

Appendix 3

List of kiln suppliers

Potclays Ltd, Brickkiln Lane, Etruria, Stoke-on-Trent.
Harry Fraser Ltd, 12 Leyfield Road, Trentham, Stoke-on-Trent.
Kilns & Furnaces Ltd, Keele Street, Tunstall, Stoke-on-Trent.
Podmore & Sons Ltd, Shelton, Stoke-on-Trent.
Fulham Pottery, 210 New Kings Road, Fulham, London, S.W.6.
Gibbons Bros Ltd, Lenches Bridge, Brierley Hill, Staffs.
British Ceramic Services Co Ltd, Bricesco House, Wolstanton,
    Newcastle-under-Lyme.
E.J. Arnold Ltd, Butterley Street, Leeds 10.
Cromartie Kilns Ltd, Dividy Road, Longton, Stoke-on-Trent.
Shelley Furnaces Ltd, Newstead Industrial Estate, Trentham, Stoke-on-Trent.
R.M. Catterson Smith Ltd, Tollesbury, Near Maldon.
Wengers Ltd, Etruria, Stoke-on-Trent.
A. Gallenkamp & Co Ltd, Technico House, Christopher Street, London, E.C.2.
James Birks Ltd, King Street, Longton, Stoke-on-Trent.
Kennedy & Sons Ltd, 12 Harcourt Street, Dublin 2, Eire.
Anna Cheyne, 30 Railway Street, Lisburn, N. Ireland.
Harrison Mayer Ltd, Meir, Stoke-on-Trent.

Index